A NavPress Bible study on the book of

GENESIS

NAVPRESS®

BRINGING TRUTH TO LIFE

OUR GUARANTEE TO YOU

We believe so strongly in the message of our books that we are making this quality guarantee to you. If for any reason you are disappointed with the content of this book, return the title page to us with your name and address and we will refund to you the list price of the book. To help us serve you better, please briefly describe why you were disappointed. Mail your refund request to: NavPress, P.O. Box 35002, Colorado Springs, CO 80935.

The Navigators is an international Christian organization. Our mission is to reach, disciple, and equip people to know Christ and to make Him known through successive generations. We envision multitudes of diverse people in the United States and every other nation who have a passionate love for Christ, live a lifestyle of sharing Christ's love, and multiply spiritual laborers among those without Christ.

NavPress is the publishing ministry of The Navigators. NavPress publications help believers learn biblical truth and apply what they learn to their lives and ministries. Our mission is to stimulate spiritual formation among our readers.

NAVPRESS, BRINGING TRUTH TO LIFE, and the NAVPRESS logo are registered trademarks of NavPress. Absence of ® in connection with marks of NavPress or other parties does not indicate an absence of registration of those marks.

ISBN 08910-9069X

Scripture quotations in this publication are from the *Holy Bible: New International Version* (NIV). Copyright © 1973, 1978, 1984, International Bible Society. Used by permission of Zondervan Bible Publishers. Other versions used are the *New American Standard Bible* (NASB), © The Lockman Foundation 1960, 1962, 1963, 1968, 1971, 1972, 1973, 1975, 1977; and the *King James Version* (KJV).

Printed in the United States of America

21 22 23 24 25 / 09 08 07

FOR A FREE CATALOG OF
NAVPRESS BOOKS & BIBLE STUDIES,
CALL 1-800-366-7788 (USA)
or 1-800-839-4769 (CANADA)

CONTENTS

HOW TO USE THIS STUDY

Objectives

Each guide in the LIFECHANGE series of Bible studies covers one book of the Bible. Although the LIFECHANGE guides vary with the individual books they explore, they share some common goals:

1. To provide you with a firm foundation of understanding and a thirst to return to the book;

2. To teach you by example how to study a book of the Bible without structured guides;

3. To give you all the historical background, word definitions, and explanatory notes you need, so that your only other reference is the Bible;

4. To help you grasp the message of the book as a whole;

5. To teach you how to let God's Word transform you into Christ's image.

Each lesson in this study is designed to take 60 to 90 minutes to complete on your own. The guide is based on the assumption that you are completing one lesson per week, but if time is limited you can do half a lesson per week or whatever amount allows you to be thorough.

Flexibility

LIFECHANGE guides are flexible, allowing you to adjust the quantity and depth of your study to meet your individual needs. The guide offers many optional questions in addition to the regular numbered questions. The optional questions, which appear in the margins of the study pages, include the following:

Optional Application. Nearly all application questions are optional; we hope you will do as many as you can without overcommitting yourself.

For Thought and Discussion. Beginning Bible students should be able to handle these, but even advanced students need to think about them. These questions frequently deal with ethical issues and other biblical principles. They often offer cross-references to spark thought, but the references do not give obvious answers. They are good for group discussions.

For Further Study. These include: a) cross-references that shed light on a topic the book discusses, and b) questions that delve deeper into the passage. You can omit them to shorten a lesson without missing a major point of the passage.

(Note: In some lessons you are given the option of outlining the passage just studied. Although the outline is optional, you will probably find it worthwhile.)

If you are meeting in a group, decide together which optional questions to prepare for each lesson, and how much of the lesson you will cover at the next meeting. Normally, the group leader should make this decision, but you might let each member choose his or her own application questions.

As you grow in your walk with God, you will find the LIFECHANGE guide growing with you—a helpful reference on a topic, a continuing challenge for application, a source of questions for many levels of growth.

Overview and Details

The guide begins with an overview of the book. The key to interpretation is context—what is the whole passage or book *about*?—and the key to context is purpose—what is the author's *aim* for the whole work? In lesson one you will lay the foundation for your study by asking yourself, Why did the author (and God) write the book? What did they want to accomplish? What is the book about?

Then, in lesson two, you will begin analyzing successive passages in detail. Thinking about how a paragraph fits into the overall goal of the book will help you to see its purpose. Its purpose will help you see its meaning. Frequently reviewing a chart or outline of the book will enable you to make these connections.

Finally, in the last lesson, you will review the whole book, returning to the big picture to see whether your view of it has changed after closer study. Review will also strengthen your grasp of major issues and give you an idea of how you have grown from your study.

Kinds of Questions

Bible study on your own—without a structured guide—follows a progression. First you observe: What does the passage *say*? Then you interpret: What does the passage *mean*? Lastly you apply: How does this truth affect my life?

Some of the "how" and "why" questions will take some creative thinking, even prayer, to answer. Some are opinion questions without clearcut right answers; these will lend themselves to discussions and side studies.

Don't let your study become an exercise of knowledge alone. Treat the passage as God's Word, and stay in dialogue with Him as you study. Pray, "Lord, what do you want me to see here?" "Father, why is this true?" "Lord, how does this apply to my life?"

It is important that you write down your answers. The act of writing clarifies your thinking and helps you to remember.

Meditating on verses is an option in several lessons. Its purpose is to let biblical truth sink into your inner convictions so that you will increasingly be able to act on this truth as a natural way of life. You may want to find a quiet place to spend five minutes each day repeating the verse(s) to yourself. Think about what each word, phrase, and sentence means to you. At intervals throughout the rest of the day, remind yourself of the verse(s).

Study Aids

A list of reference materials, including a few notes of explanation to help you make good use of them, begins on page 211. This guide is designed to include enough background to let you interpret with just your Bible and the guide. Still, if you want more information on a subject or want to study a book on your own, try the references listed.

Scripture Versions

Unless otherwise indicated, the Bible quotations in this guide are from the New International Version of the Bible. Other versions cited are the Revised Standard Version (RSV), the New American Standard Bible (NASB), and the King James Version (KJV).

Use any translation you like for study, preferably more than one. A paraphrase such as The Living Bible is not accurate enough for study, but it can be helpful for comparison or devotional reading.

Memorizing and Meditating

A Psalmist wrote, "I have hidden your word in my heart that I might not sin against you" (Psalm 119:11). If you write down a verse or passage that challenges or encourages you, and reflect on it often for a week or more, you will find it beginning to affect your motives and actions. We forget quickly what we read once; we remember what we ponder.

When you find a significant verse or passage, you might copy it onto a card to keep with you. Set aside five minutes during each day just to think about what the passage might mean in your life. Recite it over to yourself, exploring its meaning. Then, return to your passage as often as you can during your day, for a brief review. You will soon find it coming to mind spontaneously.

For Group Study

A group of four to ten people allows the richest discussions, but you can adapt this guide for other sized groups. It will suit a wide range of group types, such as home Bible studies, growth groups, youth groups, and businessmen's studies.

Both new and experienced Bible students, and new and mature Christians, will benefit from the guide. You can omit or leave for later years any questions you find too easy or too hard.

The guide is intended to lead a group through one lesson per week. However, feel free to split lessons if you want to discuss them more thoroughly. Or, omit some questions in a lesson if preparation or discussion time is limited. You can always return to this guide for personal study later. You will be able to discuss only a few questions at length, so choose some for discussion and others for background. Make time at each discussion for members to ask about anything they didn't understand.

Each lesson in the guide ends with a section called "For the group." These sections give advice on how to focus a discussion, how you might apply the lesson in your group, how you might shorten a lesson, and so on. The group leader should read each "For the group" at least a week ahead so that he or she can tell the group how to prepare for the next lesson.

Each member should prepare for a meeting by writing answers for all the background and discussion questions to be covered. If the group decides not to take an hour per week for private preparation, then expect to take at least two meetings per lesson to work through the questions. Application will be very difficult, however, without private thought and prayer.

Two reasons for studying in a group are accountability and support. When each member commits in front of the rest to seek growth in an area of life, you can pray with one another, listen jointly for God's guidance, help one another to resist temptation, assure each other that the other's growth matters to you, use the group to practice spiritual principles, and so on. Pray about one another's commitments and needs at most meetings. Spend the first few minutes of each meeting sharing any results from applications prompted by previous lessons. Then discuss new applications toward the end of the meeting. Follow such sharing with prayer for these and other needs.

If you write down each other's applications and prayer requests, you are more likely to remember to pray for them during the week, ask about them at the next meeting, and notice answered prayers. You might want to get a notebook for prayer requests and discussion notes.

Notes taken during discussion will help you to remember, follow up on ideas, stay on the subject, and clarify a total view of an issue. But don't let note-taking keep you from participating. Some groups choose one member at each meeting to take notes. Then someone copies the notes and distributes them at the next meeting. Rotating these tasks can help include people. Some groups have someone take notes on a large pad of paper or erasable marker board (preformed shower wallboard works well), so that everyone can see what has been recorded.

Pages 213-214 list some good sources of counsel for leading group studies. The *Small Group Letter*, published by NavPress, is unique, offering insights from experienced leaders every other month.

INTRODUCTION

The Book of Beginnings

"In the beginning . . . ."
Genesis 1:1

Genesis means "origin," "beginning," and the book of Genesis is about beginnings. In it, God lays the groundwork for the rest of Scripture, His revelation of Himself to man.

Genesis begins with God's creation of the world and its most blessed occupants, the human male and female. From this climax, the story follows man's plunge into rebellion and its consequences—shame, death, murder, rootlessness, tyranny, idolatry, and war. Two low points mark this account of primeval history (chapters 1-11): the Flood that wipes out an unsalvageable generation, and the scattering of the nations who try to build the Tower of Babel. Each time, man seems bound for irredeemable corruption, yet God prevents disaster with merciful judgment.

After Babel, the story narrows to follow one family—Abraham's— through four generations (chapters 12-50). Through this family, God plans to offer salvation from the consequences of the Fall to the whole human race. God calls Abraham from Mesopotamia to Canaan and promises that his descendants will own that land. In the twists of life, God teaches Abraham, his son, his grandson, and his great-grandsons to trust their Lord's promises and obey His plans. By the close of Genesis, God has led seventy members of the chosen family into Egypt but has trained them to pin their hopes on a return to Canaan four hundred years in the future. The stage is set for God's greater acts of salvation and self-revelation in the Exodus, which itself will be only a shadow of mightier things to come. Genesis constantly reminds us that it is only the beginning of a story that will climax in the New Testament and not end until the vision of Revelation is accomplished.

On the next page is a brief outline showing the four main events of primeval history and the four generations of Abraham's family.[1]

9

Genesis and the New Testament

The New Testament quotes Genesis more than any other Old Testament book except Psalms and Isaiah. The great themes of the New Testament all begin in Genesis, and many are scarcely mentioned again between Exodus and Malachi.

For instance, the garden of Genesis 2 with its river and tree of life return in Revelation, where the serpent of Genesis 3 and the Babylon built in Genesis 10-11 finally fall. A series of prophecies from Genesis 3:15 through 49:10 point toward the Christ, who transforms the consequences of Adam's sin. The New Testament God—the One personal, perfect, just, merciful, all-powerful Creator and Savior—is the God of Genesis. Likewise, the New Testament view of man's high origin and mission, and his fall and predicament, are rooted in Genesis. Grace, election, free will, the covenant relationship, the substituted sacrifice that atones for sin, the transformation of the sinner, and the obedience of faith all figure in Genesis.

Focus on redemption

Genesis doesn't tell us everything we might like to know about the history of the universe and humankind, for much of that history lies outside God's purpose in giving us the book. Genesis focuses on God's acts as they bear on His plan to redeem man from sin. The book first explains God's perfect plan for humans and then begins to trace His response to their sin—the plan of salvation through a descendant of a chosen family. The origin of the universe is relevant only in that it reveals God's character and defines man's original nature. The non-chosen branches of the human race are not unimportant to God, but they stand outside the redemption story until in Christ they ultimately receive salvation through the chosen family.

Genesis and the Old Testament

Genesis is one of the five books of Moses (see Nehemiah 8:1, John 5:46, Luke 24:27), which the Jews called the *Torah* (Teaching, Law, Instruction—Psalm

119:174, Jeremiah 31:33). The English word *Law* does not quite describe the history and instruction about God that the Torah contains. God does give rules for living, but only after He has shown His love and power by delivering Israel (the descendants of Abraham through his grandson, Jacob-Israel) from slavery in Egypt.

The Torah tells how God made a *covenant* (a treaty between a lord and his subjects) with Israel. The rest of the Old Testament recounts Israel's repeated failures to live up to God's requirements and the repeated sufferings that rebellion causes. Over and over God allows His people to suffer and learn, but He protects a remnant of the chosen family, sends prophets to warn and teach His people, and assures them that one day the promised descendant of Abraham will come. Thus, the rest of the Old Testament tells how God continues the chosen family's training, the story begun in Genesis. It takes roughly two thousand years to prepare Abraham's family to give birth to the Savior, Jesus.

Viewing the Old Testament as the story of how God shaped Israel to receive the Savior, we can see how Genesis fits into this framework:

1. The five books of Moses (Genesis, Exodus, Leviticus, Numbers, Deuteronomy) recount Israelite history from the people's beginnings until Moses' death, when the Israelites are poised on the border of the promised land (?-1400 BC). The books also give laws for living in the land under Israel's king, the Lord.

2. Nine books (Joshua-2 Chronicles) tell Israel's history from the start of the conquest of the land, through the climax of prosperity under David and Solomon, and finally to degeneration, conquest by enemies, and exile (about 1400-586 BC).

3. Three books (Ezra, Nehemiah, Esther) record history after the exile (about 538-420 BC).

4. Five books (Job-Song of Songs) give us poetry and wisdom from Israel's golden years under David and Solomon through the exile (about 1000-450 BC).

5. Seventeen books (Isaiah-Malachi) record the words of prophets from some centuries before to shortly after the exile (about 855-430 BC).

Genesis, then, is the beginning of the story. It ends with Jacob's family settled in Egypt around 1876 BC. About 430 years later, Moses led the descendants of that family out of Egypt and back to the land promised to Abraham. During the forty-year trek from Egypt to Canaan, Moses wrote Genesis and his other books. (For relative dates, see the timeline on page 16.)

Before the band of fugitive slaves entered the promised land, every one of them needed to know some core truths about their God and themselves. They had to know how being Israelites made them unique, set apart from all the peoples they were going to encounter. They needed to know who this God was who had freed them from Egypt and promised them Canaan. The stories about the Creation, the Flood, Babel, Abraham, and so on may have been passed down in Jacob's family for generations, but the people needed an accurate, written record stamped with God's authority. In Canaan, they were going to face all kinds of challenges to their calling as a holy people and to their faith in the true God, so God guided Moses to write five books to set Israel straight.

As you study Genesis, think of yourself both as a Christian and as an Israelite whose family has just entered Canaan. Keep in mind these questions: "Who is this God we've committed ourselves to? What is my relationship to Him, and how did it come about? How did our people, Israel, come to be? What did God choose us to do, and why? Where did we come from, and why are we trying to conquer Canaan?" And most importantly, "How should all this affect the way I live?"

The documentary theory

A theory current among many scholars asserts that the Torah is not the work of Moses, but rather is an edited compilation of "four types of documents, processes, or schools."[2] These four are called J (the Jahwist or Jehovah source), E (the Elohist or Elohim source), P (a Priestly school), and D (the Deuteronomist or Deuteronomic school who did the final editing). There are many variations of this theory, and also many flaws. Therefore, we will leave this debate to the commentaries[3] and follow the traditional view that Moses substantially wrote Genesis. He may have used oral and written records of tribal genealogies and history, since in societies where writing is rare, people cultivate extremely accurate memories for such things. A later editor may have updated certain place names for clarity; for instance, Dan (Genesis 14:14) was not given this name until the days of the Judges (Judges 18:29).[4] However, these details do not negate the fact that Genesis was written by Moses under the guidance of God's Spirit.

Science and Scripture

Genesis focuses on man's relationship to God and draws its information from revelation and remembered events. Science studies material remains (fossils, rocks, the stars, etc.) and repeatable experiments to answer questions about how and when things happened. Therefore, it is not surprising that science can tell us nothing about God, and that Scripture does not address technical questions of physics, chemistry, and biology. As God's Word, the Bible is infallible, but our human understanding of both God's Word and material remains is very fallible. Therefore, in this study we won't tackle alleged conflicts between traditional interpretations of Scripture and current interpretations of material remains. Instead, we will deal with the issues Genesis intends to address and ignore most others. We assume that perfect understanding of Scripture and material evidence would resolve all apparent conflicts, but these matters are unsuitable for a Bible study guide.[5]

The "Generations" of Genesis

Genesis takes its name from the Greek translation of a word that occurs ten times in the book. Most scholars now believe that the phrase, "these are the generations of . . ." (NASB, KJV, RSV) or "this is the account of . . ." (NIV) refers to the descendants of the person named and to the account that follows the statement. The ten statements structure Genesis like a family tree, as follows:[6]

Prologue (1:1-2:3)
    1:1-13   Creation's kingdoms
    1:14-31   Creature-kings
    2:1-3   Creator King
The generations of heaven and earth (2:4-4:26)
    2:5-25   Man's original blessedness
    3:1-24   Entrance of sin
    4:1-26   Man in exile
The generations of Adam (5:1-6:8)
    5:3-32   Covenant genealogy: Adam to Noah
    6:1-8   Wickedness of man
The generations of Noah (6:9-9:29)
    6:9-8:19   Covenant of the flood
    8:20-9:17   Covenant after the flood
    9:18-27   Covenant in prophecy
The generations of the sons of Noah (10:1-11:9)
    10:1-32   Origins of the nations
    11:1-9   Sin and dispersion from Babel
The generations of Shem (11:10-26)
The generations of Terah (11:27-25:11)
    11:27-15:21   Abraham inherits the covenant
    16:1-22:19   Abraham's heir: through Hagar or Sarah?
    22:20-25:11   The succession prepared
The generations of Ishmael (25:12-18)
The generations of Isaac (25:19-35:29)
    25:19-28:9   Isaac inherits and has an heir
    28:10-35:29   Jacob sojourns in Haran and returns
The generations of Esau (36:1-37:1)
The generations of Jacob (37:2-50:26)
    37:2-45:28   Jacob's heirs
    46:1-47:27   Israel's descent into Egypt
    47:28-50:26   Israel's hope of restoration

The "generations" structure keeps the story looking forward to each man's descendants, to the hope of the future.

God and man

The nineteen lessons in this guide are just an introduction to the Book of Beginnings. We will follow the main plot from two perspectives. From one angle, we will look at God—His nature and character as revealed through His words and actions. From another angle, we will look at man—who he is and should be, what God wants him to do, and what he does. We will trace God's plan of redemption through Genesis from God's side and from man's, always looking for lessons for our own lives.

The best way to begin studying a book is to read it straight through and outline it broadly for yourself. Since we expect most users of this guide won't want to read all of Genesis first, we've given you the outlines on pages 10 and 13. If you can, read as much of Genesis as possible with these outlines to guide you before beginning lesson two.

For the group

This "For the group" section and those in later lessons are meant as possible ways of organizing your discussions. Select whatever suits your group.

Worship. Some groups like to begin with prayer and/or singing. Some pray briefly at the beginning for the Holy Spirit's guidance but leave extended prayer until after the study. Others prefer just to chat and have refreshments for a while and then move to the study, leaving worship until the end. You might experiment with different structures until you find one that suits your group.

Warm-up. Many people find it hard to dive into a Bible discussion when their thoughts are still on what they did during the day. Starting with singing or prayer can help people make the transition from business to Bible study, but many groups like to begin with a brief warm-up question.

As you start a new study, whether your group has been together for a long time or has several new members, you may want to discuss what each person hopes to get out of your group—out of your study of Genesis, and out of whatever else you might do together. How much emphasis would you like to put on prayer, study, outreach to others, singing, sharing, and so on? What are your goals for personal growth, service to others, etc.? If you have someone write down members' hopes and expectations, then you can look back at these goals later to see if they are being met. Discuss what you hope to *give* as well as *get* in your group.

How to Use This Study. Make sure that the group is committed to preparing each lesson ahead of time. Point out the optional questions, the "Study Skills," and the "Study Aids" appendix on pages 211-215. If necessary, examine how members' goals for the group can be met; for instance, do you need to allow two weeks per lesson in order to save more time for prayer and sharing? Answer any questions members have about the study.

Introduction. You could do all of the preceding parts of this "For the group" when you first give members their study guides, and come the next week prepared to begin here and move to lesson one.

Here are some questions to clarify the key points of pages 9-13.

1. What does *Genesis* mean?
2. What are some of the themes of Genesis?
3. Summarize the plot of Genesis, using the four key events of chapters 1-11 and the four key men of chapters 12-50 to guide you.
4. Why does Genesis repeat the phrase "these are the generations of . . ." ten times?
5. Who wrote Genesis? Who were the author's original audience, and what were they going through at the time?
6. What does *Law (Torah)* mean? In what sense is Genesis part of God's Law?
7. How does Genesis fit into the overall message of the Old Testament and the whole Bible?

Discuss some ways in which Genesis is relevant to your lives as Christians. Why is it important for you to know the origins of the world, man, and sin? Why do Christians need to know what God promised to Abraham and his descendants, and what happened to Abraham's family?

1. J. Sidlow Baxter, *Explore the Book* (Grand Rapids, Michigan: Zondervan Corporation, 1966), volume 1, page 29.
2. James Montgomery Boice, *Genesis: An Expositional Commentary*, volume 1 (Grand Rapids, Michigan: Zondervan Corporation, 1982), page 90.
3. For a more thorough statement of the documentary theory, see John Skinner, *A Critical and Exegetical Commentary on Genesis*, second edition (Edinburgh: T & T Clark, 1956); or E. C. Blackman, *Biblical Interpretation* (Philadelphia: Westminster Press, 1957); or Gerhard von Rad, *Genesis: A Commentary* (Philadelphia: Westminster Press, 1973).

   For arguments against the documentary theory, see Derek Kidner, *Genesis* (Downers Grove, Illinois: InterVarsity Press, 1967), pages 16-26; Boice, pages 273-275; E. J. Young, *An Introduction to the Old Testament* (Wheaton, Illinois: Tyndale Press, 1964), pages 107-154; E. J. Young, *In the Beginning: Genesis Chapters 1 to 3 and the Authority of Scripture* (Edinburgh: Banner of Truth Trust, 1976); U. Cassuto, *The Documentary Hypothesis* (Magnes Press, 1961).
4. *The NIV Study Bible*, edited by Kenneth Barker (Grand Rapids, Michigan: Zondervan Corporation, 1985), page 27.
5. For more on this subject, see Kidner, pages 26-31; Boice, pages 13-77. Boice includes extensive footnotes, including *God and the Astronomers* by Robert Jastrow, *The Genesis Record: A Scientific and Devotional Commmentary on the Book of Beginnings* by Henry M. Morris, *Genesis in Space and Time: The Flow of Biblical History* by Francis A. Schaeffer, and *Creation Revealed: A Study of Genesis Chapter One in the Light of Modern Science* by Frederick A. Filby.
6. Adapted from Meredith G. Kline, "Genesis," *The New Bible Commentary: Revised*, D. Guthrie, J. A. Motyer, A. M. Stibbs, D. J. Wiseman, editors (Grand Rapids, Michigan: William B. Eerdmans Publishing Company, 1981), page 81.

TIMELINE OF GENESIS

(Dates are approximate)

	2200 BC	2100	2000	1900	1800	1700	1600	1500	1400 BC

CREATION. . . .
ADAM . . . .
NOAH . . . .

• Sargon I of Akkad

Guti invade Ur

Abraham

Isaac

Jacob

Joseph

Hittite empire founded

■ Jacob's family settles in Egypt

"Middle Kingdom" in Egypt Egypt's second greatest strength

Law code of Hammurabi in Babylon

Moses

"New Kingdom" in Egypt Egypt's greatest strength and culture

■ Exodus

■ Fall of Jericho (Joshua 6)

16

GENESIS 1:1-2:3

Heaven and Earth

Like children, most of us are full of questions. "How did the world come to be?" "Why am I here?" "What are the sun and the stars?" "Why is life so tough?" In the ancient Near East,[1] there were lots of answers to people's questions, all colored by what people wanted to believe and were able to understand.

Most ancient peoples were told various stories about the origins of the world and man, but the stories were usually meant to prove why one's own city or god was supreme (see the box, "Creation Myths" on pages 24-26). Those fantastic stories were no example for righteous life. Therefore, to prepare His people to treat Him and their fellow humans properly, the Lord had to replace a great deal of misinformation about origins. He didn't need to answer every possible question, but just enough to set the stage for the rest of His story. The first chapters of Genesis are crafted to convey key truths and overcome key errors about God, the world, and man.

Read 1:1-2:3 several times, preferably in different translations. Observe the passage's form (patterned, simple) the first time you read it. The second time through, look for the passage's content (God-centered, focusing on man and man's planet, omitting details of physics and chemistry). Notice how the form and content are relevant to God's purposes and comprehensible to almost anyone.

Formless and empty (1:2). "Without form and void" in RSV; "a waste and emptiness" in NASB mar-

17

For Further Study:
What common beliefs
in your culture con-
tradict each of the
repeated phrases in
Genesis 1?

gin. In other words, the earth had no shape or
structure, and no content.

1. a. On days 1-3, God gave form to what had been
the formless darkness of chaos. In the left
column below, write how God did this. (Observe
the repeated word "separated" or "divided" in
1:3-13.)

b. On days 4-6, God filled what had been the emptiness of chaos. In the right column below, note
how God did this on each day.

form	fullness
1	4
2	5
3	6

18

2. a. What correspondence do you see between the two sets of days?

God speaks and the world had its beginnings

b. What does this pattern tell you about God and His creation?

He is all powerful

Study Skill—Repetition

A crucial step in Bible study is *observation*— reading and rereading the passage, and observing every detail, pattern, and train of thought. Be especially alert for *repetition*, which is a clue to the ideas the author wants to emphasize. In a patterned passage like Genesis 1:1-2:3, observe as much as you can about the pattern.

3. What do you think God wants us to learn about Himself, the world, or ourselves from each of the following repeated phrases?

a. "And God said, 'Let . . . .' And it was so."

He is the creator. He spoke it into being He had a plan He is all powerful

19

Optional Application: Take time to reflect and meditate on the goodness of God's creation or on God's sovereign power in making it. You might want to do this outdoors.

For Further Study: The Apostle John began his Gospel: "In the beginning was the Word, and the Word was with God, and the Word was God. . . . Through him all things were made . . ." (John 1:1,3). Where does the Word of God appear in Genesis 1:1-3? What do you think John was claiming about Jesus by calling Him the Word? Why does John open with "In the beginning" as Genesis does? What light does John's statement throw on Genesis?

b. "it was good" (each created thing) and "it was very good" (all creation)

God does good work for our good.

4. a. What purposes or commands did God give to . . .

the sun and moon (1:16-18)? 2 great lights one to govern the day one to govern the night

the animals (1:22,26)? Waters teem w living creatures and the sky Blessed them to be fruitful and multiply

men and women (1:28)? Blessed them & said be fruitful and multiply fill the earth; Subdue it. Rule over the fish over all creatures

plants (1:29-30)? Every green plant for good

b. What can we learn about our world from the purposes God assigned to each part of His creation?

20

He provided physically
for our needs

_____

_____

_____

_____

For Thought and Discussion: How does Genesis 1 counter the following beliefs?

a. The material world, and especially the human body, is evil. Only spirit or soul is good (1:31).

b. Everything came about by chance (1:3).

c. The sun, moon, and stars determine a person's destiny (1:14-18).

d. God is a spirit or force that permeates the world. Mother Earth is divine.

e. Only male humans are created in God's image (1:27).

For Thought and Discussion: What does it mean that God made the seventh day "holy"?

For Further Study: Using a concordance, find references to the *Sabbath* and *rest* in the New Testament. How is Christ's work like the Creation (2 Corinthians 5:17, Hebrews 10:11-14)? How has Christ affected the meaning of Sabbath-rest?

Holy (2:3). Set apart for God's purposes. "Sanctified" in NASB. The Law separates things into two categories: the human/earthly/mortal/common and the holy/divine/immortal/special. There are holy meat and common meat, holy bread and common bread, holy people and common people, holy days and ordinary days. The categories teach Israel to distinguish the Holy God from all created things and all false gods, and holy Israel from the other nations. Holy things in the world (holidays, rituals, offerings) are bridges for people to experience God's holiness.

Exodus 20:11 gives Genesis 2:3 as the reason why Israel must rest from work every seventh day (compare Deuteronomy 5:15).

Study Skill—Cross-references
It is important to study the Old Testament in light of the New. *Cross-references*—other passages of Scripture—will help you do this.

5. In summary, what does 1:1-2:3 reveal about God's nature and character?

He alone created our world, all the objects - sky - earth sun, moon, stars not by chance but divinely made for his purposes and for good - 21 *for us and in us.*

The book of Revelation describes the re-creation of the world as even more glorious than the first creation. Compare Genesis 1:2-5 to Revelation 22:5, Genesis 1:6-10 to Revelation 21:1, and Genesis 1:14-19 to Revelation 21:23. What do you observe?

Optional Application:
a. According to Romans 1:20-21, how should humans respond to God's revelation of Himself in creation?

b. What happens to those who don't respond like this (Romans 1:21-32)?

c. What do these observations imply for your life?

For Further Study:
Hebrews 11:1-3 tells one lesson we can learn from Genesis 1:1-2:3. What is that lesson?

Study Skill—Application

Second Timothy 3:16-17 says, "All Scripture . . . is useful for teaching, rebuking, correcting and training in righteousness, so that the man of God may be thoroughly equipped for every good work." Therefore, the last step of Bible study is asking yourself, "What difference should this passage make in my life? How should it make me want to think or act?" Application will require time, thought, prayer, and perhaps even discussion with another person.

You may sometimes find it more productive to concentrate on one specific application, giving it careful thought and prayer, than to list several potential applications without really reflecting on them or committing yourself to them. At other times, you may want to list many implications that a passage has for your life. Then you can choose one or two of these to act or meditate upon.

---

6. a. What is the most significant thing you learned about God, man, or the world from Genesis 1:1-2:3?

Gods power so powerful he spoke everything into being

b. What are some implications this truth has for your life?

That I need to remember His power, He is creator I am creation he molds us into what he wants us to be

c. Is there some specific way in which you can apply this insight to your thoughts and/or

22

actions this week or this month? Or, is there some specific change in your outlook you would like to consistently pray about and look for ways to apply? If so, write down your plans.

Let Him do as he Pleases with my life and be obedient. Itully surrendered to Him.

Optional Application: How should Genesis 1:1-2:3 affect the way we treat the land, plants, and animals in our world?

Take care of it — not ruin it.

7. If you have any questions about anything in this study, list them here. Plan to raise them in your group meeting, or ask another Christian.

For the group

Warm-up. Ask each person to share one aspect of creation that amazes him or her.

Reading aloud. It is usually a good idea to read the passage silently or aloud just before discussing it. This reading refreshes everyone's memory. You won't be able to do this in later lessons when you are covering several chapters, but you could have one person or several people read 1:1-2:3 at this point.

Questions. In even the best Bible study guide, you will sometimes find a question unclear. However, you can usually reduce any question to one of three basic questions: What does this passage tell us about God—who He is and what He does? What does it tell us about man (or woman)? What does it tell us a Christian should do? The question will normally be asking you either to *observe* what the passage says, *interpret* what it means, or *apply* it to yourselves.

Keeping these guidelines in mind as you work through the lesson will help you to rephrase the questions in interesting ways. For example, instead of asking, "What did you get for number 3?" you can ask, "What does 'Let there be light . . . And it was so' tell you about God?" Let several people respond. Then ask, "What does 'Let . . .' tell you about our world?" If no one answers, follow up with, "What other explanations for the origin of light have you heard?" Some people claim that light energy has always existed, and others worship energy or the sun as God.

Many groups feel that half their discussion time should be devoted to exploring how the passage applies to their lives. If you've prepared the interpretation questions ahead of time, you should not need long to cover them. But even if you decide to spend less than half your time on application, do allow at least fifteen minutes for it. Don't insist that members *do* something about the passage, but do encourage them; ask what difference it should make to their lives. You could suggest that each member tell one person outside the group one significant insight he or she had from your discussion. Or, suggest that a member choose an insight or several verses to meditate on for the next week.

Summarizing. Ask one person or several people to summarize the main points of your discussion. What do you want to remember from 1:1-2:3? Summarizing a discussion helps to clarify it in people's minds and helps them remember it.

Worship. You could choose songs that focus on God the Creator. Praise Him for His creation, and thank Him for the purposes He gave to man and woman. Your applications may lead you to topics for prayer. Ask God to enable you to live in light of what you have studied.

Creation Myths

The accounts in Genesis 1-4 have been called "myth," but experts on myth agree that Genesis

(continued on page 25)

(continued from page 24)

is very different from what is usually called myth,[2] as we can see if we compare Genesis 1 to other ancient stories.

Five Egyptian cities had five different accounts of the origin of the world, the gods, and man. Each myth was designed to prove that its city was the place where creation began and that its god was supreme. The stories varied, but each portrayed creation as a birth process from single gods or male-female couples. The gods embodied such forces as air, moisture, earth, sky, and sun.

Likewise, Babylon's creation account, *Enuma Elish*, was written to show how Marduk became the chief god of Babylon. The myth was used for magical recitation to influence natural events.[3] To get the flavor of how Babylonians conceived of gods and man, consider this summary:

"In the beginning there were two gods, Apsu and Tiamat, who represented the fresh waters (male) and marine waters (female). They cohabited and produced a second generation of divine beings. Soon Apsu was suffering from insomnia because the young deities were making so much noise; he just could not get to sleep. He wanted to kill the noisy upstarts, despite the protests of his spouse, Tiamat. But before he managed to do that, Ea, the god of wisdom and magic, put Apsu to sleep under a magic spell and killed him.

"Not to be outdone, wife Tiamat plotted revenge on her husband's killer and those who aided the killing. Her first move was to take a second husband, whose name was Kingu. Then she raised an army for her retaliation plans.

"At this point the gods appealed to the god Marduk to save them. He happily accepted the challenge, on the condition that if he was victorious over Tiamat, they would make him chief of all gods.

"The confrontation between Tiamat and Marduk ended in a blazing victory for Marduk. He captured Tiamat's followers and made them his slaves. Then he cut the corpse of Tiamat in half, creating heaven from one half of it and the

(continued on page 26)

(continued from page 25)

earth from the other half. He ordered the earlier supporters of Tiamat to take care of the world.

"Shortly thereafter, Marduk conceived another plan. He had Kingu killed and arranged for Ea to make man out of his blood. In the words of the story, man's lot is to be 'burdened with the toil of the gods.' To demonstrate their gratitude to Marduk, the gods then helped him to build the great city of Babylon and its imposing temple."[4]

Notice that the Babylonians could not imagine creation without a male and female god, for they thought gods were like humans. Observe also that, unlike Israel's God, the gods needed companionship, food, and sleep (compare Psalm 121:4), and had selfish rather than loving, moral motives. Man was an afterthought, created from the blood of a rebel god to be a slave. These were the notions current in Abraham's and Moses' day that the Lord needed to refute.[5]

The Babylonian story is wordy and elaborate, while Genesis 1 uses "only 76 different word forms fundamental to all mankind, arranged in a wonderful poetical pattern yet free from any highly colored figures of speech."[6] It is intelligible to any child, yet includes all the essential facts of creation.

1. The "Near East" is more or less what is often called the "Middle East": Turkey, Syria, Palestine, Jordan, Arabia, Egypt, Iraq, and Iran. The maps on pages 80 and 90 show this region with the place names Genesis uses.
2. C. S. Lewis, "Faulting the Bible Critics," *Christian Reflections* (Grand Rapids, Michigan: William B. Eerdmans Publishing Company, 1967), quoted in Boice, page 130. See also Fred Gladstone Bratton, *Myths and Legends of the Ancient Near East* (New York: Thomas Y. Crowell Company, 1970), pages 1-14, 36-41, 57-64.
3. Waltke, page 47.
4. J. I. Packer, Merrill C. Tenney, and William White, Jr., editors, *The World of the Old Testament* (Nashville: Thomas Nelson Publishers, 1982), pages 110-112.
5. Packer, Tenney, and White, pages 112-113.
6. Frederick A. Filby, *Creation Revealed: A Study of Genesis Chapter One in the Light of Modern Science* (Westwood, New Jersey: Fleming H. Revell, 1963), pages 15-16.

GENESIS 1:26-29, 2:4-25

Male and Female

Chapter 1 told how God created the earth and shaped it to accommodate its ruler—the human race. The rest of Genesis will focus on that last and chief of God's earthly creations.

The Babylonian myth *Enuma Elish* told people they were made as an afterthought to feed and work for the gods (see page 26). Modern doctrines teach that humans evolved by chance from lower life forms and may still be evolving into greater forms. However, Genesis 2 answers these false claims to set God's people straight. Genesis 1:1, 2:4 is a topic sentence summarizing 2:4-4:26. Genesis 1:2, 2:5-6 tells the state of things before God begins the work at hand.

The story begins just before the sixth day of creation and focuses on important information about man's place in the world.[1] Read 1:26-29 and 2:4-25 to see what man and woman were before they fell. Look for clues to these two questions: "Who am I?" and "What should I do?"

LORD God (2:4). The name "God" in Genesis usually translates the Hebrew word *Elohim*. This is a title; it designates a holy, divine being as opposed to a mortal. Actually, the word is a plural as well as a unity, usually called the plural of majesty.[2] The plural signifies "the One who completely possesses all the divine attributes."[3] Elohim is God the Creator who transcends His creation and inhabits eternity.

27

For Thought and Discussion: a. What beliefs about man's origin have you heard that contradict Genesis 1:27, 2:7?

b. What beliefs about man's nature and purpose have you heard that contradict Genesis?

For Further Study: How is man like (1:22,28,29-30; 2:7,19) and unlike (1:24,26,28; 2:19,20) animals?

The Hebrew word rendered "LORD" in NIV is *YHWH*, the personal name of the true Creator God. Some versions of the Bible render this name "Jehovah" or "Yahweh," but we do not know how it was pronounced because the Jews considered it too holy to be spoken. YHWH means "I AM" (Exodus 3:14); that is, not just "I exist" but "I am actively present"[3] (compare Isaiah 8:10). YHWH is God intimately with His creation.

Sometimes Genesis uses just God's title (Elohim, as in 1:1-2:3), sometimes it uses just His name (YHWH, as in 4:1-16), and sometimes it uses both (YHWH Elohim, as in 2:4-3:24).

Man (2:7). "The Hebrew for *man* (*adam*) sounds like . . . the Hebrew for *ground* (*adamah*); it is also the name *Adam* (see Genesis 2:20)."[4] The Hebrew *adam* normally means "human, mankind" as opposed to "male."[5] The connection between "man" and "dust of the ground" stresses man's creatureliness (2:7) and later his brief life (3:19).[6]

Living being (2:7). The same phrase as "living creature" in 1:20 and 1:28. KJV and a NASB marginal note read "living soul." Both man and animals are living creatures.

1. Genesis asserts that man came into being by a decision and act of God (1:26, 2:7). What can we learn from the following passages about man's original nature and character?

1:26-27 _We were made in the image of God to rule the things of this world._

2:7 _We were born from the dust of the earth and given Gods breath of life_

28

2:25 _Had no shame at this point - free_

Name (2:19). In the ancient world, the right to name something or someone indicated rule or ownership.[7] God named day, night, seas, etc. (1:5,8,10). (See also 2:23; 4:25; 17:5,15.)

2. What do these passages tell you about humanity's intended purpose and task?

1:26,28 _To be care takers of all God had made_

2:15 _To work the earth and take care of it._

2:19-20 _God He included man by allowing him to name creatures as of having ownership._

3. In what senses is man made in God's image (1:27)? (How do man's abilities and function on earth reflect God's image?)

We are to take on His character, to be care takers of this earth

For Thought and Discussion: According to Genesis 1-2, does a person's worth come from what he does, or from something else? How might this fact affect the way you treat yourself and others?

For Thought and Discussion: What do 2:15,20 and 3:17-19 tell you about what work was supposed to be and how it changed after man sinned? Why do we work?

For Thought and Discussion: What guidelines did God give man for ruling and subduing the earth (1:29, 2:15-17)?

Optional Application: What does being made in God's image imply for the way you approach your life? How could your life better reflect His image? (Consider Luke 20:22-25.)

For Further Study:
What are two moral implications of the fact that we are made in God's image (Genesis 9:6, James 3:9)?

For Thought and Discussion: Can we learn anything about God from the fact that He expressed His image in male and female?

Optional Application: How might being "one flesh" with your husband and his "suitable helper" affect how you act? Or, how might you treat your wife as "one flesh" with you and your "suitable helper"?

_____
_____
_____
_____
_____

Sin has blurred (Colossians 3:10, 1 John 3:2) but not erased the image of God in us.

4. God made the female human in some ways like and in some ways unlike the male. What does 1:26-27 tell you about what woman is and how she is related to man?

Made in God's image
according to His likeness
given dominion over all for
of these kinds of things, an
all creeping things.
both

5. What does 2:21-23 tell you about woman's nature and relationship to man? (What is the significance of woman having been made from a part of man?)

Bone of my bone
flesh of my flesh
And she shall be called
Woman
Because she was taken
out of man

Helper (2:18,20). Scripture often uses this word for God (Hosea 13:9, Psalm 115:9-11) and occasionally for military allies ("staff" in Ezekiel 12:14), so "helper" does not imply inferiority in itself.[8] The sense is more of a needed ally than a servant girl. This helper is God's last, greatest gift to man (compare the other gifts in 2:1-18) and the climax of Genesis 2.[9]

6. The woman was given rule over the rest of earth's creatures along with the man (1:26-28). The woman's task was to be a "suitable helper" (2:18,20), something only the man's own flesh could be. Consider 1:28; 2:15,18,24. What do you think a suitable helper was meant to be and do?

fruitful: multiply
tend: keep the garden
a helper: work together
joined together to
be one flesh.

For Thought and Discussion: What implications do Genesis 1:26-27 and 2:4-25 have for Christian marriage?

Optional Application: Does Genesis 1-2 suggest that God is concerned about people? What difference do your observations make to you?

For Further Study: Study how God's re-creation of the world will be like but even better than what Genesis 2 describes (Revelation 21:3-5, 22:1-5). Why is this important to know?

Eden (2:8). Related to a Hebrew word meaning "bliss, delight" or a Mesopotamian word meaning "a plain."[10]

A river (2:10). This mammoth river, greater than any river now existing, was the source of the two great rivers on which Babylon and other kingdoms relied in Moses' day—the Tigris and the Euphrates (2:14). The Greeks called the region _Mesopotamia_, "the land between the two rivers" because the people's livelihood depended on those rivers. However, in Eden's time, those great rivers were mere branches of a greater one. Eden must have been somewhere in Mesopotamia (modern Iraq), perhaps near Ur. (See the map on page 80.)

7. What can we learn about God from the way He provided for man a garden, a mighty river, many trees for food, and a suitable helper in his work (2:8-24)?

that he is one provider
knows our needs

31

For Thought and Discussion: Genesis 2:24 stresses that a *man* must leave his parents and does not mention a woman leaving. Why is it so important to remind husbands to leave parents emotionally? Is this important for wives also? Why or why not? Is this relevant to your marriage? If so, how?

For Thought and Discussion: Paul says that Genesis 2:24 is a reason why sex outside marriage is a perversion of God's intent for people (1 Corinthians 6:15-17). How does extramarital sex pervert Genesis 2:25?

_____

_____

_____

_____

Leave his father and mother (2:24). In Moses' day, a person's loyalty to his or her parents was strongly emphasized. The patriarch (father) of an extended family was its leader and expected loyalty from his sons and daughters. A man's loyalty to parents could easily conflict with his commitment to his wife, but God established two laws to govern this conflict: Genesis 2:24 and Exodus 20:12.

Study Skill—Application

It can be helpful to plan an application in five steps:

1. Record the verse or passage that contains the truth you want to apply to your life. If the passage is short enough, consider copying it word for word, as an aid to memory.

2. State the truth of the passage that impresses you. For instance:

   a. *"Everyone I know is made in God's image (1:27). That image involves uniqueness, value, creativity, personhood, the capacity to love and relate, moral responsibility, authority that derives from God, etc."*

   b. Or, *"My wife is my suitable helper (2:20). She is made in God's image like me; she is my ally, partner, right-hand person, crucial to the work God has given me."*

3. Tell how you fall short in relation to this truth. (Ask God to enable you to see clearly.) For example:

   a. *"I don't have much respect for Bernard. I don't treat him as a grand and significant creature bearing God's image. I tend to dismiss him."*

(continued on page 33)

(continued from page 32)

      b. *Or, "Martha and I have a generally good relationship, but I tend to think of her work and my work, rather than our joint ministry. I don't make maximum use of the abilities God gave her."*

4. State precisely what you plan to do about having your life changed in this area. (Ask God what, if anything, you can do. Don't forget that transformation depends on His will, power, and timing, not on yours. Diligent prayer should always be part of your application.) For instance:

      a. *"I will have lunch with Bernard this week and really listen to him. I'm going to pray for true respect for him. James 3:9 reminds me also to watch what I say to and about Bernard."*

      b. Or, *"I'm going to talk to Martha about how she and I can be better partners in the work God has given us. I'm going to carefully consider her opinions. We'll discuss and pray about how I can help (or let) her be my helper."*

5. Plan a way to remind yourself to do what you have decided, such as putting a note on your refrigerator or in your office, or asking a friend or relative to remind you.[11]

8. a. What truth from 1:26-29 or 2:4-25 would you like to apply to your life this week? Write down the verse reference, and explain the truth in your own words. (Use one of the "Optional Application" questions in this lesson, if you like.)

Have more respect for my husband. Listen better. Work together more

b. How do you fall short in this area? Or, what general implications does this truth have for your life?

Tend to not listen, be respectful.
Remember he too was created in God's image.

c. Is there any specific step you can take toward living more in accord with this truth? After praying about this, write down any plans you have.

Ask God to help me trust him more

d. How can you see to it that you remember to do this?

Prayer

9. If you have any questions about 1:26-29 or 2:4-25, record them here.

For the group

Warm-up. What does the modern secular world, or other philosophies and religions you know, teach about what a human being is? What is our purpose, according to those views? (Don't spend more than a few minutes discussing this. A warm-up question is intended only to get the group thinking, and this one is meant only to provide ideas to contrast with the biblical view of man.)

Read aloud.

Summarize. Basically, what is 2:4-25 about? Why is this passage important for us to study? What does it have to do with the aims of Genesis—such as explaining to God's people who they are and what their relationship to God is?

Questions. The explanation about Elohim and YHWH on pages 27-28 shows two aspects of God: transcendent Creator, and immanent (near) Lord and Helper. Draw attention to these two aspects of God, which we need to hold in tension together. Advocates of the documentary theory (see page 12) claim that the different names for God point to sources with different theological views, but other scholars refute this conclusion.

For group discussion notes, you might use three large sheets of paper. On one sheet, write what you learned about *God* from 1:26-29 and 2:4-25, with verse references to keep yourselves tied to the text at hand. On the second sheet, write what you learned about *mankind* (both male and female). Divide the third sheet into two columns, one for what you learned about *man* (the male) and one for *woman*.

The roles of men and women are hot topics today, so answers to questions 4-6 may vary widely. Pray that group members will grow in love and understanding for each other even if they disagree. Pray also that they will base their views on Scripture, not bend Scripture to support either conservative or liberal views learned from their culture.

Share your answers to question 8, and give everyone the opportunity to ask questions about how to apply Scripture. Some people may feel shy about sharing their personal applications. If so, respect one another's privacy. You may have to demonstrate your trustworthiness to each other for some time before everyone feels ready to reveal private things. Still, you don't need explicit details about each other's private lives to be able to support each other's applications with prayer and counsel. Resist the temptation to turn the sharing of applications into a chance for gossip and unwanted advice.

Summarize. Sum up your discussion briefly.

Wrap-up. In preparation for Genesis 3:1-24, ask the group to compare 2:4-25 to the world you live in. Ask everyone to look for similarities and differences.

Worship. Praise God for the loving care He reveals in 2:4-25. Thank Him for the way He made you. Ask Him to enable you each to fulfill the applications you have planned.

1. Albert H. Baylis, *On the Way to Jesus* (Portland, Oregon: Multnomah Press, 1986), page 32.
2. *The NIV Study Bible,* page 6.
3. J. A. Motyer, "The Names of God," *Eerdmans' Handbook to the Bible*, edited by David Alexander and Pat Alexander (Grand Rapids, Michigan: William B. Eerdmans Publishing Company, 1973), page 157.
4. NIV footnote to 2:7.
5. J. I. Marais, "Anthropology," *The International Standard Bible Encyclopaedia*, volume 1, edited by James Orr (Grand Rapids, Michigan: William B. Eerdmans Publishing Company, 1956), page 145.
6. Hewart Vorlander, "Man," *The New International Dictionary of New Testament Theology*, volume 2, edited by Colin Brown (Grand Rapids, Michigan: Zondervan Corporation, 1976), page 564.
7. Baylis, page 34; *The NIV Study Bible,* page 6.
8. Bruce K. Waltke, "The Relationship of Sexes in the Bible," *Crux,* number 19 (September 1983), pages 10-16.
9. Baylis, pages 33-34,36-39.
10. *The NIV Study Bible,* page 9.
11. This "Five-point Application" is based on the method in *The 2:7 Series*, Course 4 (Colorado Springs, Colorado: NavPress, 1979), pages 50-51.

GENESIS 3:1-24

Paradise Lost

Genesis 1:1-2:25 paints the world as ordered, balanced, and "very good." Man was made in God's image to govern and cultivate the earth in God's name. But our world is full of violence, decay, and death, and men are immoral abusers of the land and creatures. What happened? Genesis 3:1-24 explains.

Look back at the outlines on pages 9 and 13, and recall the themes of Genesis from pages 9-14. Then read 3:1-24, looking for the overall point of the story. Observe the character traits that the humans and God each display.

Study Skill—Tracing Themes and Purposes
The outlines on pages 9 and 13 can help you see Genesis as a whole. However, another aid toward grasping the book's overall messages is a chart or outline that relates each section to the main themes and purposes of the book. You can make such an outline as you go along, revising your statement of themes and purposes when necessary.

You can begin such an outline of Genesis like this:
Purpose of Genesis: To show Israel who God is, how Israel came to be His people, and what He has chosen Israel to be and do.
    (1:1-11:26) Primeval History
        (1:1-2:25) The original situation: God's good creation.

(continued on page 38)

For Further Study:
If you like, begin your own outline of Genesis according to the model on pages 37 and 38. Use separate paper.

(continued from page 37)

(1:1-2:3) God is the Creator of heaven and earth; no other gods helped Him, and He is not part of His creation. He made man, male and female, in His image to rule His creation under Him. The world God made was very good.

(2:4-25) God is an abundant giver, and He loves His creatures. He originally gave man blessed circumstances, fulfilling work, and whole relationships with earth, animals, partner, and God. (These gifts contrast with life as we know it, so the question "why?" arises.)

1. If you were to add 3:1-24 to the outline begun above, what would you say? How does 3:1-24 contribute to the themes of Genesis?

> *Man has fallen - made very poor choices - cursed for being given unto sin - Removed from the Garden - to toil; Endure hardships*

The tree of the knowledge of good and evil (2:9,17). It isn't clear what this tree was, but the command in 2:16-17 was apparently the only restriction God gave Adam. The knowledge of good and evil (which may mean moral knowledge or discernment[1]) seems at first glance to be a necessary and desirable possession (see Genesis 3:22, Deuteronomy 1:39, 1 Kings 3:9, Hebrews 5:14). However, for reasons of His own, God forbade it.

Derek Kidner believes that to speculate on the exact knowledge this tree conveyed and how it imparted this knowledge is to repeat Eve's mistake. Eve felt she had a right to decide for herself whether the command was reasonable, but God wanted her to trust His judgment. Like Eve, we are told only that God empowered many trees in the garden to nourish human bodies—these were "pleasing to the eye and good for food" (2:9)—and one tree to inform human minds (see 3:6).[2]

The tree of life (2:9, 3:22). Most commentators agree that this was a second tree, and many believe it was or symbolized Christ. Again, we are not told how it was supposed to impart life; we assume that both trees figured in God's loving intentions for His people. Observe that God did not forbid man from eating of the tree of life in 2:17. For further study, see Revelation 2:7; 22:2,14.

Serpent (3:1). In many ancient cults, the serpent "was a symbol of deity and fertility, and the images of serpent-goddesses have been found in the ruins of many Canaanite towns and temples."[3] Moses' Israelite audience knew what the serpent meant to other nations, and Israel also knew that pagan gods were either demons or delusions exploited by demons. Therefore, the Israelites would have come to the same interpretation that the New Testament gives: the serpent was Satan in disguise (John 8:44, Romans 16:20, Revelation 12:9).

The serpent was a real creature, not just a symbol of evil or human weakness in a myth about every man's encounter with temptation. Later pagan legends and rites about the serpent-goddess who gives power show this creature at the same work.[4]

For Thought and Discussion: God showed Adam no reason for the command in 2:16-17. What might God's purpose have been in giving the man a command without an explanation?

For Thought and Discussion: God promised that Adam would die if he ate from the forbidden tree (2:17). Why was death the necessary result of disobeying God? (See John 1:4, Acts 17:28.)

Study Skill—Interpreting Old Testament Narratives, part one

A narrative is a story, but the Genesis narratives are *true* stories about what God and man did long ago. The biblical narratives are meant to glorify God, teach us about Him, and teach us how to live. Gordon Fee and Douglas Stuart offer several guidelines for interpreting biblical narratives.

1. "A narrative does not usually directly
(continued on page 40)

For Thought and Discussion: What do you think the man should have done when the woman offered him the fruit?

(continued from page 39)
teach a doctrine."

2. "An Old Testament narrative usually illustrates a doctrine or doctrines taught propositionally elsewhere." (The Apostle Paul explains the doctrines of the Fall, Original Sin, and the Atonement in chapters 3-5 of his letter to the Romans.)

3. "Narratives may teach either explicitly" (by clearly stating something; Genesis 3:17) "or implicitly" (by clearly implying something without actually stating it). *Implicit* does not mean *hidden.* We infer Adam's attitudes from his words (question 6), but we do not look for mystical meanings in the story. Be wary of teachers who reveal the "true" meanings of scriptures that most Christians don't see.[5]

2. The temptation of Eve gives us insight into some of the schemes with which the enemy also attacks us.

a. What was the serpent trying to achieve by asking "Did God really say . . ." (3:1)?

   Doubt Gods word

b. How might a modern person experience a similar temptation?

   Doubt the Bible as God's word

c. What is the proper response to such a question (Psalm 19:7-14, 119:11, Luke 4:4 [Deuteronomy 8:3])?

40

law   testimony

The Lord's perfect, and
statutes
right   his commandments pure
fear of the Lord is clean enduring forever
His word is living is life
To be obeyed
To hide in my heart.

Observe the contrast between what God really said
and did and what Eve said in reply to the serpent's
question:

God	Eve
"You are *free to eat* from *any* tree in the garden" (2:16)	"We may eat fruit from the trees in the garden" (3:2)
"In the middle of the garden were the tree of life and the tree of the knowledge of good and evil" (2:9)	"*the tree* that is in the middle of the garden" (3:3)
"you must not eat from the tree of the knowledge of good and evil" (2:17)	"God did say, 'You must not eat . . . and *you must not touch it'*" (3:3)[b]

3. Eve forgot the tree of life and focused on the
   forbidden tree as *the tree*. She weakened God's
   lavish provision of so many trees from which
   she was *free to eat* to keep her from being
   hungry or bored. And she amplified God's prohi-
   bition to include even *touching* the tree.
      What conclusions about Eve's attitude
   toward God can you draw from these
   observations?

We change things in
our mind our
perception is
deceived.

41

For Thought and Discussion: Satan claimed that eating the fruit would make Eve like God (3:5). In what way was this true (3:22)? In what way was it a deception?

4. a. Eve's reply (3:3) shows that Satan's first scheme worked. Observe his next words (3:4-5), and describe his second tactic to alienate Eve from God.

You shall not surely die, striving to make her desire to be like God. Full of Knowledge

b. How might a modern person experience this temptation?

Lust after the things of this world including Knowledge —

c. How should Eve have responded to the serpent?

Fled from there

5. a. Three good things—nourishment, beauty, and wisdom—attracted Eve to the fruit (3:6). What was wrong with pursuing these good things through the fruit?

They are false and only monetary.

b. How might a modern person make the same mistake?

People after fame,

42

m died, or
such.

For Thought and Discussion: From this story, how would you define sin?

For Further Study: How did the sin of the earth's governors affect the earth (Genesis 1:28, 3:17, 9:2; Romans 8:19-23)? How will Christ restore what sin marred?

6. The couple's actions and words in 3:7-13 reveal how knowing good and evil affected their inner natures. Why did they . . .

want to cover themselves (2:25, 3:7)?

O r due d their eyes were
opened and they felt
shame; guilt and
needed to cover it.

hide from God (3:8-10)?

Guilty, done wrong,
How often we do
the same.

each shift blame to someone else (3:12-13)?

We are always blaming
Others for what we
alone have allowed to
happen through disobedience

7. Observe what happened to the man and woman because of their sin (3:16-24). How were their lives and tasks now different from their original state? (Compare 1:26-28; 2:7,15,18-25.)

man's life and work (3:17-19) *had*
work of the soil
sweat of the brow
fruit of the bush

For Thought and Discussion: God said man would die when he ate the fruit. The serpent said he would not die. Which spoke the truth? How do you know? (See 3:7-10,19,22; 5:5.)

until he dies &
returns to dust

woman's life and work (3:16) _____

multiply in some
conceiving, birthing
children in pain.
Ruled by one
mates.

relations between man and woman (3:12,16)

Blaming each other
not taking our own
sin & being responsible

relations between humans and God (3:10,23)

hide from God
driven from his original
blessing

Clothed them (3:21). Nakedness now signified shame, which the humans were unable to cover (2:25, 3:7). Some commentators find it significant that the covering of shame required an animal's death—a foreshadow of the sacrificial system to atone for (cover) sin.

8. What do you learn about God from the ways He responded to sin and sinners?

For Thought and Discussion: What evidence does 3:21-24 show of God's plan to restore His creatures to their intended purposes?

3:9,11,13 _He smight us, question, made us accountable._

3:14-15 _He made us accountable pay for our sins by consequences_

3:16-19 _punished_

3:21 _provided_

3:22-24 _Took us out of the garden his original plan for man – to strive because of our sin._

Offspring (3:15). "Seed" in KJV. Genesis 3:15 is a prophecy of Christ, the offspring of Eve who has crushed Satan and undone the effects of his temptation. Satan bruised Jesus in His crucifixion, but Jesus crushed Satan by canceling sin and so destroying Satan's power of death (Hebrews 2:14-15).

For Further Study:
Study in Romans and 1 Corinthians what it means to be "in Christ" versus "in Adam." How has Christ undone each of the effects of Adam's sin—enmity, sin, death, toil, etc.? To what extent do we already experience the restoration Christ accomplished, and to what extent do we await the fulfillment of that restoration? (See 1 Corinthians 13:12; 2 Corinthians 3:18, 5:17; Ephesians 2:11-18; 1 John 3:2. Or, consider these questions as you study the New Testament in the future.)

Romans 5:12-19 and 1 Corinthians 15:20-26 further explain how Christ overcame Adam's sin. As head of the human race, Adam passed on to his descendants his status as God's enemy and his bent toward rebellion. But Christ became the "second Adam," the representative head of all people who ally with Him.

Study Skill—Application

As Christians, we have the Holy Spirit of God to help us resist the serpent and forsake the sins of Adam and Eve. For ways of responding to the Spirit's offer of help, see Jesus' model in Luke 4:1-13. See also Romans 8:5-13 and 1 John 1:8-10.

9. a. Are you like Adam or Eve in any ways? If so, name one area in which you would like to change.

prone to rebel-

b. What prayer and/or action could you pursue this week to be more the person God desires you to be? (If necessary, write down a plan for reminding yourself as well.)

Lord I lay down self I want not to always be the rebel. You are changing me Lord. Day by Day. Forgive me in my slowness. Thank you Lord

46

10. Consider what you learned about God from the way He dealt with the first human sinners. Are you moved to respond in prayer and/or action? If so, how?

Sorry Adam & Eve choose to listen. Sorry we repeat it today even when we have your holy spirit. to guide us.

Optional Application: Does 3:1-24 lead you to any response—such as confession, thanksgiving, praise, request, asking forgiveness from another person, forgiving someone, changing an attitude, or resisting a temptation?

11. List any questions you have about 3:1-24.

For the group

Warm-up. Let each person name one way in which people and our world are different today from the way Genesis 2 says God made them.

Read aloud.

Summarize. Question 1 should help with this. Encourage the group to make outlines as you go along. You might periodically compare the strengths and weaknesses of each other's outlines.

Questions. The questions focus on how Satan tempted Eve (and tempts us), how Eve and Adam sinned (as we sin), and how their sin affected them and their world (us and our world). Try to identify with Eve and Adam at each stage. Then look at what the chapter reveals about God's character. Finally, consider how Christ has overcome the effects of sin.

Question 8 may be difficult for some. If necessary expand on it with questions like these: Why did God clothe the sinners instead of leaving them naked and ashamed? Why did He curse the serpent and the ground rather than Adam and Eve? Why did He banish them from the garden, multiply their toil and pain, and sentence them to death? Why would it have been terrible for them to live forever without being reconciled to God? What does the promise of 3:15 tell you about God's feeling for His human creatures?

Discuss several possible answers to questions 9 and 10 to serve as models for group members who still find application difficult. If you learned anything from trying to apply chapter 2, share your insights.

We've broken the Study Skill on interpreting narratives into parts to give you less to absorb at any one time. If you prefer to discuss it all at once, you can find the four parts on pages 39, 63, 91, and 101. Review these guidelines frequently, and look for ways to apply them to your study of Genesis.

Worship. Thank God for not destroying mankind when Adam and Eve sinned. Thank Him that from the beginning He planned a solution to their problem. Praise Him for remaining perfectly just while perfectly merciful and loving. Ask Him to enable you to resist temptation this week.

1. Baylis, page 49; Geerhardus Vos, *Biblical Theology* (Grand Rapids, Michigan: William B. Eerdmans Publishing Company, 1948), pages 39-43; H. C. Leupold, *Exposition of Genesis*, volume 1 (Grand Rapids, Michigan: Baker Book House, 1942), pages 120-121.
2. Kidner, pages 62-63.
3. Nahum M. Sarna, *Understanding Genesis* (New York: Schocken Books, 1966), page 26.
4. Baylis, pages 50-51.
5. Gordon Fee and Douglas Stuart, *How to Read the Bible for All Its Worth* (Grand Rapids, Michigan: Zondervan Corporation, 1982), pages 73-74, 78, 83.
6. Baylis, page 51.

GENESIS 4:1-5:32

Man in Exile

Sin killed Adam spiritually; he lost the capacity to be intimate with God and the freedom to escape the state of sin (Ephesians 2:1-2). Spiritual death corrupted man's soul, so that his reason, emotions, and will became flawed. Eventually, Adam faced physical death, the last ravage of the cancer of sin.

Adam's children inherited his disease. Genesis 1-2 revealed God's intent for man, in chapter 3 man shattered that intent, and now in Genesis 4-11 we see the depths to which man plunged in his flight from God. In these chapters, watch for the repeating cycle of sin, judgment, and mercy.

The line of Cain (4:1-26)

What is life like when you have rejected God's garden? Genesis 4 shows the tragic path of Cain's descendants, but Genesis 5 points toward another hope. Read 4:1-26 prayerfully, for the overall point of the chapter.

An offering to the LORD (4:3). Adam's family was not totally alienated from God. People could no longer be with God intimately, face to face, but they could pray to Him and acknowledge their dependence on Him for life. According to the Law of Moses, offerings of animals, grain, and other produce could express thanks to God for

49

For Further Study:
For Further Study:
How does the need
for an atonement
offering explain
Christ's work?

**Optional
Application:** Evalu-
ate your own thoughts
about God and your
brothers in light of
Cain's example. Does
your worship please
God?

providing fertility and other blessings (Leviticus
2:1-16, 23:9-21; Deuteronomy 16:9-17, 26:1-11).
However, only animal offerings could *atone for*
(literally, "cover") guilt as clothing covered
nakedness (Genesis 3:21). An evildoer deserved
death (Genesis 2:17), but God accepted a blood
sacrifice in place of a human death (Leviticus
1:4, 4:1-5:13).

Some people think that Cain's and Abel's
offerings were meant to atone for sin, and that
God rejected Cain's because grain could not
atone. Other people believe the offerings were
for thanks, worship, and devotion, and that God
rejected Cain's because of his inner attitudes.[1]

1. What is 4:1-26 about?

_____

_____

_____

_____

2. What wrong attitudes in Cain might have made
   God reject his act of worship (Genesis 4:3-7;
   Hebrews 11:4; 1 John 2:9, 3:12)?

_____

_____

_____

_____

_____

_____

Study Skill—Names In Scripture
Ancient people believed that a name had
power because it expressed the essence of
the thing or person named. The right to name
someone was authority to pronounce his
(continued on page 51)

50

(continued from page 50)
nature and destiny (Genesis 2:19). Names were often prophetic.

Many, but not all, of the names in Scripture can tell us about the people they name. For instance:

Adam = *dust* (2:7)
woman = *of/from/like man* (2:23)
Eve = *living, life-giver* (3:20)
Cain = *spear* or *smith* but sounds like *acquire* or *get* (4:1)
Abel = possibly *breath, vapor*

Notice that the name may only sound like a significant word, and that it may have a double meaning. For example, Eve named Cain "acquire" because she was grateful to have acquired him, but he showed the character of one bent on acquiring throughout his life (4:3-7,17). Abel's name "breath" may point to his brief life or his attention to spiritual things.[2]

For Further Study: Compare Genesis 4:3-7 to Isaiah 1:10-20, Jeremiah 7:21-24, and Amos 5:21-24. Under what circumstances does God reject acts of worship?

For Thought and Discussion: Did Cain have a right to be angry in 4:5? Why or why not (4:6-7)?

3. Describe how Cain treated God in . . .

4:5 _____

_____

_____

_____

4:7-8 _____

_____

_____

_____

4:9 _____

_____

_____

_____

4:13-14 _____

_____

For Thought and Discussion: Did Cain repent of his sin (4:13-14)? How can you tell?

Optional Application: Are you your brother's keeper (4:9)? Specifically what does your answer imply for your responsibilities?

4. What do you learn about Cain's character from the way he treated and spoke of his brother (4:8-9)?

_____

_____

_____

_____

_____

5. Do you in any ways treat God or other people as Cain did? If so, how?

God _____

_____

_____

_____

_____

others _____

_____

_____

_____

_____

_____

City (4:17). "The Hebrew for this word can refer to any permanent settlement, however small. Cain tried to redeem himself from his wandering state by the activity of his own hands—in the land of wandering he builds a city."[3]

52

6. a. Cain's attitudes toward God and man landed him in the situation of 4:12-17. What happened to Cain?

_____

_____

_____

_____

_____

b. How is modern life without God like Cain's situation?

_____

_____

_____

_____

_____

7. a. Does the story of Cain suggest any matters for prayer, repentance, and/or action on your part? If so, what insight is relevant?

_____

_____

_____

_____

_____

b. How do you need God's help in this area? (*Optional:* See Ephesians 3:16-21, Philippians 2:12-13.)

_____

_____

_____

_____

_____

Optional Application: a. Does Cain's story motivate you to seek any growth in the ways in which you treat God or people? If so, describe the character quality you would like to acquire.

b. Write down any first steps you can take toward acquiring this quality, by God's grace.

c. What are your plans for prayer and/or action?

_____

_____

_____

_____

_____

_____

8. What aspects of His character does God display
   in . . .

   4:5 _____

   _____

   _____

   4:6-7 _____

   _____

   _____

   4:10-12 _____

   _____

   _____

   _____

   4:15 _____

   _____

   _____

9. What signs of humanity's decay do you observe
   in Cain's descendants?

   4:19 (compare 2:24) _____

   _____

   _____

   _____

4:23-24 _____

_____

_____

_____

_____

For Further Study:
Compare Lamech's oath about vengeance (Genesis 4:24) to Jesus' command that we forgive a brother 77 times (Matthew 18:22). How does fallen human nature differ from Christlike character?

Seven . . . seventy-seven (4:15,24). Seven was the number of completeness or perfection in Hebrew idiom, perhaps because of 2:3.

Study Skill—Types in the Old Testament

A *type* is an Old Testament person, object, or event that God designed to resemble its antitype in the New Testament. God gave types to prepare Israel to understand Christ, and to be moral and doctrinal examples for us (1 Corinthians 10:6,11; Hebrews 10:1). In some cases the New Testament explicitly states that something in the Old Testament is a type (Hebrews 7:3, 9:8-9, 11:19; 1 Peter 3:21). At other times it does not. Some interpreters have fallen into error by abusing typology, but we can avoid foolish mistakes if we keep some principles in mind.

1. "No doctrine or theory should ever be built upon a type or types independently of direct teaching elsewhere in Scripture." Types are meant to illustrate, amplify, and illuminate doctrines taught explicitly elsewhere.

2. "The parallelism between type and antitype should not be pressed to fanciful extremes." For instance, Adam differs in some important ways from Christ, although he is a type of Christ (Romans 5:14). Cain is a type of the worldly, self-centered man, but we probably shouldn't conclude that farming, wandering, or building cities are inherently less godly than herding flocks.[4]

55

For Thought and Discussion: What were Seth and his descendants appointed to be? (See 3:15.)

For Thought and Discussion: Why does Moses repeat 1:26-27 in 5:1-2? What point does this information serve in this new context?

Optional Application: How can you grow more like Abel and Enoch, as Hebrews 11:4-6 describes them? What situations in your life are calling for this kind of faith?

Seth (4:25). Cain's line shows the descent of corrupt man from Adam, but this corruption didn't prevent God from pursuing His plans (4:25-26). Seth's name means "appointed"[5] or "granted."[6]

The line of Seth (5:1-32)

Read chapter 5, noting its pattern and some important exceptions to that pattern. Notice also the key truths about mankind that 5:1-2 repeats.

This is . . . Adam's line (5:1). Or, "This is the book of the generations of Adam" (KJV, NASB). Recall the outline on page 13. The Cain branch of Adam's line was summarized in chapter 4 and set aside, for only the Seth branch survived the judgment in Noah's day (6:5-9).

10. What is 5:1-32 about?

_____

_____

_____

_____

_____

_____

11. The refrain "and then he died" echoes through chapter 5. What truth should this echo drive home for us (2:17, 3:4)?

_____

_____

_____

_____

_____

12. a. Enoch alone leaves the story differently: "He was no more, because God took him away" (5:24). What do you think the phrase "God took him away" means? (See also Hebrews 11:5-6.)

_____

_____

_____

_____

_____

b. Why did Enoch receive special treatment? (Explain from Genesis 5:24 and Hebrews 11:5-6.)

_____

_____

_____

_____

_____

_____

c. What New Testament promise does Enoch's experience point toward (1 Corinthians 15:50-57)?

_____

_____

_____

_____

_____

For Further Study: Keep a list of the notes of hope in Genesis, such as 3:15 and 5:24.

Optional Application: What implications does the promise in 1 Corinthians 15:50-57 have for your present life?

Methuselah (5:27). The name may mean "When he is dead, it shall come."[7] Methuselah's 969th year was the year of the Flood (5:25,28; 7:6).

57

For Further Study:
Review the Study Skill
on pages 37-38, then
add 4:1-26 and
5:1-32 to your outline
of Genesis.

Study Skill—What's the Point?
Every Old Testament narrative is on three levels: it is an individual episode; it is part of
Israel's history; and it is part of God's ongo-
ing history of redemption. A narrative like
Genesis 5:1-32 may not have a moral of its
own, but it is important as part of Israel's history or the story of fall and redemption.

Another clue to seeing the point of a narrative is asking, "How does this passage
relate to what comes before and after it?"[8]

The genealogies (family trees) of Genesis may bore us, but each one has a purpose
in the overall message of the book. For more
on genealogies, see page 60.

13. What do chapters 4 and 5 contribute to the
message of Genesis?

chapter 4 _____

_____

_____

_____

_____

chapter 5 _____

_____

_____

_____

_____

14. Write down any questions you have about
4:1-5:32.

_____

_____

For the group

Warm-up. These days it is popular to say that man is basically good, and that only society, parents, or bad laws psychologically wound him. Ask members each to name one sign of the Fall in their world. (Let anyone pass who prefers not to answer.)

Read aloud. Instead of reading all of 4:1-5:32 at once, read just 4:1-16 and discuss questions 1-8. Then read 4:17-26 and discuss question 9. Instead of reading 5:1-32 for questions 10 and 11, you could read only 5:1-5,21-23,28-32.

Summarize. Summarize each section (4:1-16, 4:17-26, 5:1-32) as you come to it. Questions 1 and 10 ask you to summarize the *content* of each chapter in preparation for studying it, whereas question 13 asks you to state the *point* of each chapter by relating it to the book as a whole. If you try to summarize both the content and the point of each chapter before discussing the chapter in detail, you will lay good groundwork for your discussion. You can always revise your summaries after more discussion.

However, if the group can't answer question 13 at the beginning, come back to it at the end. Try rephrasing it: What does the descent of Cain contribute to our understanding of the state from which the promised offspring (3:15) needed to free mankind? What does the account of Seth's line contribute to this? (Notice that the descent of Cain focuses on *sin* and the line of Seth focuses on *death.*) Why do we need to know that Noah was descended from Adam (who bore God's likeness, 5:1) through Seth (who bore Adam's likeness, 5:3)? How do Cain's and Seth's lines contrast each other? What do they have in common? Why is it important to know that Adam begat Seth, who begat Noah, who begat Abraham, who begat David, who begat Jesus (as Luke 3 points out)?

The line of Cain. You may want to read about *atonement* in a Bible dictionary, Bible encyclopedia, or dictionary of theology, in case anyone wants to know more about why the Old Testament sacrifices were needed and how Christ fulfilled that need. Groups with more time may want to discuss the Study Skills on pages 50, 55, and 58. Look for ways to apply these guidelines.

However, the focus of questions 2-7 is on Cain's sinful character as a model in which you can recognize yourselves and from which you can repent. Likewise, question 9 shows further sins to avoid. At the same time, don't overlook what God reveals about Himself (question 8).

The line of Seth. Don't dwell too long on chapter 5, but do make sure that everyone sees the chapter's purpose. First Thessalonians 4:13-18 is also relevant to question 12c.

Worship. This lesson is full of the "bad news" that the "good news" of Jesus overcomes. Confess to God that Genesis 4-5 is a true picture of you and your world, and thank Him for what He has done about it. Pray for your fallen world and your friends living Cain's unhappy life. Songs about the world's grief and Jesus' victory might be appropriate.

Partial Genealogies?

If we add up the ages of the men named in 5:1-32 and 7:11, we get a total of 1,656 years from Adam's creation to the Flood. However, the *Septuagint* (the Greek translation of the Old Testament that was used in the apostles' day) gives different figures that add up to 2,242 years, and the Samaritan Old Testament's figures add up to 1,307 years. This variation alone makes "it impossible to fix a definite date for Adam."[9] A similar variation occurs among manuscripts of 11:10-26.[10]

However, it was common in ancient times to include only landmark names in genealogies. For example, Matthew 1:8 says that Joram begat Azariah, but we know from 2 Kings 8-15 that Joram (Jehoram) begat Ahaziah, who begat Joash, who begat Amaziah, who begat Azariah (Uzziah). Matthew selected names to yield 2 x 7 generations from Abraham to David, 2 x 7 from David to the

(continued on page 61)

(continued from page 60)

exile, and 2 x 7 from the exile to Jesus. Multiples of seven occur frequently in ancient genealogies.

Cain's line (Genesis 4:17-18) includes six men, a number signifying humanity or imperfection. Cain's line plus Adam gives seven names.[11] Each of the six names in 4:17-18 parallels one of the names in 5:1-32:

Cain - Kenan (5:12)
Enoch - Enoch (5:21)
Irad - Jared (5:18)
Mehujael - Mehalalel (5:15)
Methushael -Methuselah (5:25)
Lamech - Lamech (5:28)

This parallelism suggests that Moses selected names from two longer genealogies to emphasize that the lines of Cain and Seth were parallel but contrasting. From Adam to Noah in 5:1-32 includes a round ten generations, just as from Shem to Abram in 11:10-26. Ten was another popular number for genealogies because it, too, signified completeness.

Another piece of evidence that encourages scholars to think Moses recorded only partial genealogies is that adding up the numbers in Genesis 11:10-26 would date the Flood only around 2500-2600 BC. However, Egyptian and Mesopotamian written records extend back to about 3000 BC.[12] If Moses omitted several generations, the dates do not conflict.

It's important to remember that omitting names from genealogies was standard practice, not dishonesty, in Moses' day. The lists in Genesis serve their purpose of tracing family connections whether they are complete or not, although they may not allow us to date the Flood and the Creation.[13]

1. M. O. Evans, "Abel," *The International Standard Bible Encyclopaedia*, volume 1, page 5. See also Boice, pages 201-202.
2. Baxter, page 66; F. K. Farr, "Cain," *The International Standard Bible Encyclopaedia*, volume 1, pages 538-539.
3. *The NIV Study Bible*, page 12.
4. Baxter, pages 55-56.
5. Kidner, page 78.
6. NIV footnote to 4:25.
7. Boice, page 232.

8. Fee and Stuart, pages 74-75,93.
9. Packer, Tenney, and White, page 57.
10. Packer, Tenney, and White, pages 53-54.
11. *The NIV Study Bible*, page 12. Some people have tried to reduce all the numbers in the Bible to arcane symbolism of this sort. Most scholars recognize the symbolism of the numbers of names in genealogies, but they take other biblical numbers literally.
12. Packer, Tenney, and White, pages 52-54.
13. Among the books from an evangelical perspective that regard the Genesis genealogies as partial are Packer, Tenney, and White, pages 53-54; *The NIV Study Bible*, pages 12-13; Kidner, pages 82-83; Boice, page 233. Boice footnotes other sources.

GENESIS 6:1-9:17

The Flood

Adam and Eve had many children (5:4), and after
many centuries their descendants were numerous
(6:1). Most of them resembled the heirs of Cain, but
one godly line, the family of Seth, remained a spark
of hope in the gathering darkness. From Adam to
Lamech onward (4:1-24) man's plunge into corruption accelerated, until at last the degeneration
reached a crisis (6:1-8). To see what God did about
this crisis, read 6:1-9:17.

**Study Skill—Interpreting
Old Testament Narratives, part two**
    4. "*All* narratives are selective and
incomplete. Not all the relevant details are
always given (see John 21:25). What does
appear in the narrative is everything that the
inspired author thought important for us to
know."
    5. "Narratives are not written to answer
all our theological questions. They have particular, specific, limited purposes and deal
with certain issues, leaving others to be dealt
with elsewhere, in other ways."[1]

Sons of God (6:2). Some commentators think these
    are fallen angels, sent by Satan to corrupt the
    human race and prevent the birth of the Savior.[2]
    Others think the sons of God are the sons of

63

For Thought and Discussion: a. When Paul says in Romans 3:23 that all people fall short of God's glory, does Paul mean that we are 70% or 80% good but not good enough? In light of Genesis 6:5 and 8:21, what does Paul mean?

b. What are some reasons that might lead a person to disagree with Genesis 6:5? Other than simply asserting the authority of Scripture, how would you try to unconvince someone who thinks people are essentially good?

For Thought and Discussion: Explain Genesis 6:6 in light of 1 Samuel 15:28-29,35. What does 6:6 reveal about God?

Seth as opposed to those of Cain.[3] Derek Kidner concludes that Scripture doesn't give us enough information to identify the sons of God for certain, and that the point of 6:1-8 is the same whoever the sons of God are.[4]

My Spirit . . . years (6:3). The Hebrew here is obscure. God is announcing either a) "the period of grace between God's declaration of judgment and its arrival would be 120 years" or b) "man's life span would henceforth be limited to 120 years (but see 11:10-26)."[5]

Nephilim (6:4). Another cryptic word. It may mean "giants" as KJV translates it.[6] Or, it may mean "fallen ones."[7] The Nephilim seem to be the offspring of the sons of God and the daughters of men.

1. Many of the details of Genesis 6:1-8 are obscure. Still, what is the clear main point of the passage?

_____

_____

_____

_____

_____

_____

The flood covenant with Noah (6:9-8:22)

Favor (6:8). Or, "grace."[8] There is no indication that Noah earned God's favor.

Righteous (6:9). "Just" in KJV. This word includes a right relationship of humility and obedience toward God, as well as the just, upright actions that follow from that relationship. Hebrews 11:7 asserts that Noah was accounted righteous because of his faith in God.

Blameless (6:9). "Perfect" in KJV. God regarded Noah as righteous. Likewise, Noah's neighbors considered him ethically blameless. He wasn't sinless, but his contemporaries found no fault with his actions because he took morality seriously.

2. Because of God's favor, Noah became righteous and blameless even in the midst of a depraved generation.

   a. How are Christians able to act righteously and blamelessly (Philippians 1:9-11, 2:12-15)?

   _____

   _____

   _____

   _____

   _____

   _____

   b. Describe one opportunity you have to act righteously in the midst of your generation.

   _____

   _____

   _____

   _____

   _____

   _____

Covenant (6:18). A covenant is simply a treaty, pact, or contract between two individuals. Archaeologists have found many secular covenants from biblical times. The ones God makes in the Old Testament resemble covenants that a king would make with his subjects. Some ancient covenants include acts of loyalty and obedience the subject must do in return for the sovereign's protection. Other covenants are unconditional grants from a sovereign to a loyal servant.[9]

3. Explain the covenant God made with Noah before the flood (6:13-7:5).

_____

_____

_____

_____

_____

_____

Ark (6:14). In 6:14-16, God describes a box 450 x 75 x 45 feet, the size of some modern ocean liners and with proportions suitable for excellent floating and maximum storage, not for sailing speed. G. F. Wright calculates that after storing enough food to support several thousand pairs of animals on a voyage of a year, there would remain more than fifty cubic feet for each pair.[10]

Noah built this huge ark "in a dry, land-locked region where it was inconceivable that there would ever be enough water to float the vessel."[11]

Noah's family stayed in the ark a total of 370 days.[12]

4. Hebrews 11:7 commends Noah for his "faith." From Hebrews 11:1,7 and Genesis 6:9-8:20, record all the ways Noah showed faith in God.

_____

_____

_____

_____

_____

_____

_____

_____

_____

_____

5. a. Hebrews 11:7 also commends Noah's "holy
   fear." What is holy fear?

   _____

   _____

   _____

   _____

   b. How did Noah display this trait (Genesis
   6:9-8:20)?

   _____

   _____

   _____

   _____

   _____

6. What other good qualities of Noah do you
   observe in 6:9-8:20?

   _____

   _____

   _____

   _____

   _____

Optional Application: Meditate this week on Hebrews 11:7, and look for ways in which your circumstances call for Noah's character traits.

For Further Study: Read 1 Peter 3:18-22 and Romans 6:3-4. How is Noah's experience a type of Christian baptism?

7. How can you act in faith, holy fear, or another of Noah's traits in the circumstances you are facing?

_____

_____

_____

_____

_____

_____

_____

The covenant after the Flood (9:1-17)

Covenant (9:9). This covenant resembled a "royal grant" in which a king granted some benefit "to a loyal servant for faithful or exceptional service. The grant was normally perpetual and unconditional, but the servant's heirs benefited from it only as they continued their father's loyalty and service."[13]

  Because this is a new beginning for the human race and all creatures, God repeats some of what He told Adam.

Sign (9:12). "A covenant sign was a visible seal and reminder of covenant commitments. Circumcision would become the sign of the covenant with Abraham (see 17:11), and the Sabbath would be the sign of the covenant with Israel at Sinai (see Exodus 31:16-17)."[14]

8. With whom did God covenant after the Flood (9:9-10)?

_____

_____

_____

9. Name the stipulations of this covenant.

a. God's side (9:11) _____

_____

b. man's side (9:1) _____

_____

(9:2-3) _____

_____

(9:4-6) _____

_____

c. the sign that guaranteed the covenant
(9:12-17)

_____

For Thought and Discussion: Why do you suppose God now allowed men to eat meat?

Lifeblood (9:4). In ancient times, blood was a potent symbol and embodiment of life, and God affirmed that "the life of every creature is its blood" (Leviticus 17:14). Pagans drank blood to acquire its life-force and used blood in magical rites to sustain life and fertility.

---

10. What is wrong with eating blood to acquire its life-force for oneself? How does this offend God?

_____

_____

_____

_____

_____

_____

11. Why did God command the death penalty for murder (9:6)?

_____

69

Summary

12. How is 6:1-9:17 related to the events of 1:1-5:32?

_____

_____

_____

_____

13. a. In 8:21-22 and 9:14-16, God promises never again to destroy all the earth's creatures. What problem does this merciful decision leave unsolved (3:6-7, 8:21)?

_____

_____

_____

_____

b. The rest of Genesis and the Old Testament points toward God's ultimate solution to that problem. What is this ultimate solution (Genesis 3:15, Isaiah 53:4-6, Romans 5:17-19)?

_____

_____

_____

_____

_____

_____

For Further Study:
Add 6:1-9:17 to your
outline of Genesis.

14. What does the story of the Flood and the remnant's deliverance tell you about God (His
nature, personality, values, etc.)? See especially
6:5-8,11-13,18-21; 7:1; 8:1,15-22.

_____

_____

_____

_____

_____

_____

_____

15. a. What aspect of God's character in 6:1-9:17 is
most encouraging or challenging to you right
now?

_____

_____

_____

_____

_____

b. How is this aspect relevant to your life?

_____

_____

_____

_____

_____

c. Does this aspect of God move you to respond with any prayer or action? (Consider what you wrote in questions 2 and 7.) If so, explain.

_____

_____

_____

_____

_____

_____

_____

16. List any questions you have about 6:1-9:17.

_____

_____

_____

_____

For the group

Warm-up. There are many good songs about the Flood. You might begin with one, and then have someone retell the story of 6:1-9:17. Perhaps a different person could recount each chapter. It might be fun to notice how the song has changed the story. (One popular song says Noah built the ark out of hickory bark. Hickory was more familiar to the song's first singers than was the biblical "cypress" or "gopher wood.")

Summarize. Use questions 12 and 13 as a foundation for the rest of your discussion. Relating the passage to the rest of the book is hard for many people, so you may need to give help. First, how is 6:1-9:17 related to 1:1-5:32? (The downward spiral of sin reaches a crisis; God responds with judgment for the many and redemption for the righteous few. Israel's history repeats this pattern often; see Isaiah 10:20-23 and Romans 11:1-7.)

Second, how does 6:1-9:17 contribute to the theme of Genesis, God's plan to overcome the effects of the Fall through the chosen family of Abraham? (Destroying all but a remnant is not a final solution. God plans to save mankind through one of Noah's descendants—Jesus.)

Questions. Try not to get sidetracked onto the mysteries of 6:1-8; just summarize the plain point the passage is meant to make, and refer questioners to the footnotes in the lesson.

Refer people who want to discuss the historicity of the Flood to Boice's book. He discusses the feasibility of the ark holding 35,000 species of animals, evidence for the Flood, etc., and he gives other sources.

Focus your discussion on what the flood story tells us about God, His plan of redemption, man's fallen character, judgment, and the example Noah sets for us. Notice the twin themes of judgment and redemption, justice and mercy.

Wrap-up. As usual, have someone summarize your discussion. You might plan to begin your next meeting by sharing how your commitments to apply Genesis to your lives have been going. Ask each person to come prepared to tell one chance he or she has had to put into practice a lesson learned from Genesis 1-9. If someone finds he hasn't successfully practiced anything from Genesis, he might tell how he could have done so, but didn't. Or, a member might share how things she's learned about God have affected her prayer life. A person's most lasting application might be just a new way of looking at who God is and what a human being is—the doctrines of God and man have far-reaching implications for our moral, social, and political views.

Rather than a time to boast or feel condemned, this could be a chance for members to air questions and frustrations about applying Scripture, especially the Old Testament. People should not expect dramatic changes in each other in three weeks.

Worship. Thank God for His patience with mankind despite our corruption, and for the gift of Christ, our Ark. Ask God to show you how to act with Noah's character in your circumstances, and to enable you to do so.

Other Flood Accounts

The Babylonian Epic of Gilgamesh records that the gods caused a worldwide flood because men and women had become intolerably wicked. A ship in the shape of a perfect cube was provided to save some people and animals. After seven days of rain, a raven, a dove, and a swallow were sent out of the ship one at a time to see whether the waters had receded. When the people were finally able to land, they offered a sacrifice of thanks to the gods, who accepted it and covenanted never again to destroy the earth in this way. Scholars agree that differences of detail and outlook show that the Babylonian and biblical flood stories are independent accounts of the same incident.

The Gilgamesh story is the best known of several hundred stories of an ancient worldwide flood collected by Tim LaHaye and John Morris in *The Ark on Ararat.* This book lists 17 flood stories from Africa and the Middle East, 38 from the Pacific Islands, 21 from the Far East, 13 from Europe and Asia, 21 from Greek authors, 58 from North America, 21 from Central America, and 24 from South America. Among these accounts, 88% record a favored family saved for its righteousness, while many others name unrelated survivors. Animals are saved in 67%. Seventy percent say that the survivors spend the flood in a boat, and 57% say that the survivors end up on a mountain. Human wickedness leads to the flood in 66%. Smaller percentages mention birds sent out, a rainbow, and exactly eight people saved.

The accounts in the Middle East are most like the biblical one, while the stories vary more and more the further they are from the Middle East. This fact leads LaHaye and Morris to conclude, "The universal Flood traditions can only have come from a common source, embellished with local color and culture, but retaining enough pertinent data to convey both historical and moral concepts."[15]

1. Fee and Stuart, page 78.
2. Boice, pages 244-249. See also Kidner, pages 83-84, citing Job 1:6, 2:1, 38:7; Daniel 3:25; 1 Peter 3:19-20; 2 Peter 2:4-6.

3. Baxter, pages 39-41; John Murray, *Principles of Conduct* (Wheaton, Illinois: Tyndale House, 1957), pages 243-249.
4. Kidner, page 84.
5. *The NIV Study Bible*, page 14.
6. Kidner, page 85.
7. *The NIV Study Bible*, page 14.
8. On "favor," "righteous," and "blameless," see Boice, pages 255-258.
9. J. A. Thompson, *Deuteronomy: An Introduction and Commentary* (London: InterVarsity Press, 1974), page 18; *The NIV Study Bible*, page 19.
10. G. F. Wright, "Ark of Noah," *The International Standard Bible Encyclopaedia*, volume 1, page 246.
11. *The NIV Study Bible*, page 1872.
12. For a chronology of 7:6-8:14, see Charles F. Pfeiffer, *The Book of Genesis* (Grand Rapids, Michigan: Baker Book House, 1958), page 32; or Kidner, pages 98-99.
13. *The NIV Study Bible*, page 19.
14. *The NIV Study Bible*, page 18.
15. Boice, pages 282-288.

Nations descended from Noah's sons

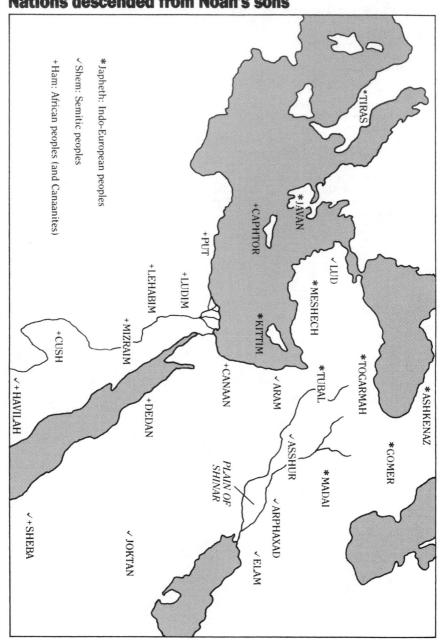

* Japheth: Indo-European peoples
✓ Shem: Semitic peoples
+ Ham: African peoples (and Canaanites)

* TIRAS
* JAVAN
+ CAPHTOR
+ PUT
✓ LUD
* MESHECH
* LUD
+ LEHABIM
+ LUDIM
+ MIZRAIM
+ CUSH
✓ + HAVILAH
* KITTIM
+ CANAAN
✓ ARAM
* TUBAL
* TOGARMAH
* ASHKENAZ
* GOMER
+ DEDAN
✓ ASSHUR
PLAIN OF SHINAR
* MADAI
✓ ARPHAXAD
✓ + SHEBA
✓ JOKTAN
✓ ELAM

GENESIS 9:18-11:26

The Scattering of Noah's Descendants

The Flood was not a permanent solution for sin because the eight human survivors inherited Adam's flaws. So for a final solution, God's focus shifted to a single branch of the family of one of Noah's sons. However, before turning to the line of Shem, Moses quickly covered the other descendants of Noah. (Recall how he dealt briefly with Cain's line in 4:1-24 before tracing Seth's.) These people were still important to God; He would ultimately save the descendants of Ham and Japheth through the chosen Shemites.

Read 9:18-11:26. The map on page 76 shows probable early territories of the nations named in 10:2-32. The locations are based on ancient documents and inscriptions that mention the nations' names. In general, the descendants of Shem are Semitic (including Arabs), the Japhethites are Indo-Europeans, and the Hamites are Africans and the now-extinct Canaanites. On the map, notice that the three spheres of Asia, Europe, and Africa meet at a tiny strip of land—Canaan, now called Palestine.

Noah's sons (9:18-29)

Moses' original audience were the Israelites poised on the border of Canaan. God had commanded Israel to conquer the land and enslave or massacre all the Canaanites (Deuteronomy 7:1-6). What could possibly justify this harsh treatment? Genesis 9:18-29, along with what we know of Canaan, offers a clue.

For Thought and Discussion: Was righteous Noah sinless (9:20-21)? Why is this fact important for our understanding of Genesis, and of what it means to be righteous?

For Further Study: Review the Study Skills on pages 37, 39, and 58. How do any of them help you to interpret 9:18-11:26?

Optional Application: Have you ever scoffed at your father (Genesis 9:22)? Why is this so serious (Exodus 20:12, Ephesians 6:1-3)?

1. What was sinful about Ham's deed (9:22)?

_____

_____

_____

_____

_____

Cursed be Canaan! (9:25). Noah prophetically cursed Ham's son for Ham's sin. God ordained that this son alone would inherit the worst of his father's character and bear the consequences of his depravity. Canaanite literature and archaelogical remains reveal that Canaan's religion "included child sacrifice, idolatry, religious prostitution and divination."[1] God expressly forbade Israel to copy Canaan's religious and sexual ways (Leviticus 18:2-30; Deuteronomy 7:1-6, 12:1-3, 18:9-12), for He was destroying Canaan for these practices (Deuteronomy 9:4-5).

Lowest of slaves (Genesis 9:25). Joshua enslaved the Gibeonites (Joshua 9:27) and other Canaanites (Joshua 16:10). Some Canaanites resisted Israelite rule for centuries (Judges 1:27-36) until Solomon subdued all of them (1 Kings 9:20-22). However, Israel's sin made this victory brief; Israel succumbed to Canaanite religion and morals, and eventually other Shemite nations—Assyria and Babylon—conquered the land. The Canaanites were destroyed permanently, but Israel was not the victor.

Some people have claimed that Ham's African descendants were also ordained to serve Europeans and Asians. However, only Canaan, a Caucasian (white- or tan-skinned) race, was cursed.[2]

Live in the tents of (Genesis 9:27). Share in the blessings of Shem. This blessing on Japheth was not fulfilled until the western Gentiles were brought into the Shemite (Semitic) covenant with the Lord in New Testament times.[3]

78

2. Why is 9:18-29 important for the overall story of Genesis and the Bible?

_____

_____

_____

_____

_____

_____

For Thought and Discussion: Why is it significant that Noah called the Lord "the God of Shem" (9:26)?

For Thought and Discussion: What does 10:1-32 contribute to the story of Genesis?

Nations descended from Noah's sons (10:1-32)

Does Genesis 9:18-11:26 describe a legendary time unknown outside the Bible? Far from it; archaeology can sketch us a firm outline of those centuries between the Flood and the time of Abraham.

The oldest known towns and villages can be dated back to at least 7000 BC; at that time Jarmo in Mesopotamia was a village, but Jericho in Canaan had a "massive stone wall"[4] around it. By 4000 BC, there were cities at Ugarit, Nineveh, and other places in the biblical world. Noah's descendants were already spreading south from Ararat and planting farm communities with walls and wells.

Each community developed its own cult and dedicated itself to the god of the cult. "Soon the cult virtually owned the community."[5] Agricultural gods and goddesses were worshiped in rituals timed to the cycle of seasons.

Eventually, communities began to unite under one cult with one priest-king and one temple. Temple-towers have been found in Shinar, Egypt, and Elam; the tower of Babel (Genesis 11:1-9) was perhaps the most ambitious of these. Those early religious states invented arithmetic to record economic transactions and astrological observations, and writing for legends, songs, poems, laws, and ethics.[6]

As wealth and populations grew, the early states expanded. Egypt united around 2800 BC, and the pyramids were begun around 2600 BC.[7] Elam and Mesopotamia also grew into empires.

The Near East

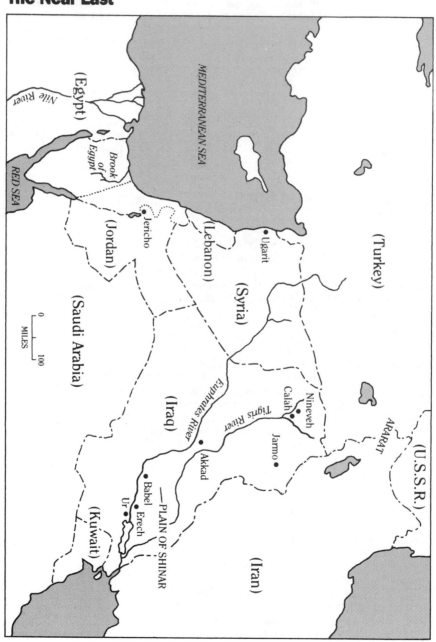

Genesis 10:8-12 tells us that Nimrod founded the first "kingdom"—a state in which someone rules a group of unrelated people, as opposed to a clan of families—in Mesopotamia. Nimrod's kingdom included the Babel (Babylon) of Genesis 11:1-9 as well as other cities on the map on page 80.

Nimrod was also the first "mighty warrior," a fact the Bible mentions three times. Martin Luther believed this meant that Nimrod was the first despot who conquered men by force of arms. Donald Grey Barnhouse translates Genesis 10:9a, "He was an arrogant tyrant, defiant before the face of the Lord."[8]

Some scholars think that Nimrod was the same person as Sargon I of Akkad, who conquered Mesopotamia around 2300 BC.[9] Sargon built roads, began a postal service, and collected a library of thousands of clay tablets.[10]

The tower of Babel (11:1-9)

This event occurred before the nations of chapter 10 spread far, for 11:1-9 explains why the nations scattered with different languages (see 10:5). The story is more than a fanciful tale, for it reflects practices known from archaeology. Yet, this turning point in man's plunge into sin has lessons for us.

The structure of 11:1-9 is a key to understanding it.[11] The story is built like an hourglass:

    11:1-2 narrative
    11:3-4 discourse ("Come, let's . . .)
    11:5   turning point
    11:6-7 discourse ("Come, let us . . .)
    11:8-9 narrative

3. Compare 11:1-2 to 11:9. What has changed?

_____

_____

_____

_____

_____

_____

For Further Study:
a. Trace what Babylon symbolizes in the rest of Scripture—Isaiah 13:1-14:23, 47:1-15; Jeremiah 20:1-6, 25:1-14, 50:1-51:64; Revelation 18:1-24.
b. Compare Nimrod's "great city" (Genesis 10:12) and Babel's temple-tower with Jerusalem, the City of God in Revelation 21:1-22:5.

Shinar (11:2). The plain between the Tigris and Euphrates rivers, called Sumer outside the Bible. See 10:10, 14:1 and the map on page 80.

Bricks . . . tar (11:3). Stone and mortar were the building materials of Canaan, but because stone was scarce in Mesopotamia, "mud brick and tar were used (as indicated by archaeological excavations)."[12]

Tower that reaches to the heavens (11:4). Many temple-towers were built in Mesopotamia between 2800 and 2200 BC. Their names show that they "were meant to serve as staircases from earth to heaven: 'The House of the Link between Heaven and Earth' (at Larsa), 'The House of the Seven Guides of Heaven and Earth' (at Borsippa), 'The House of the Foundation-Platform of Heaven and Earth' (at Babylon), 'The House of the Mountain of the Universe' (at Asshur)."[13]

The Babylonians developed the zodiac and horoscope in order to learn and control human destiny by reading the stars. Their chief gods were the sun, the moon, and the five known planets. The temple-tower called *Birs Nimroud* at Babylon, which still exists in ruins, was a staircase-hill with a tower on top for astrological readings and rites. The structure was 153 feet high and covered nearly four acres. It was built of mud bricks and tar in seven stages, and was painted to correspond to the sun, moon, and planets: the lowest stage or stair is black for Saturn, the next is orange for Jupiter, and so on. The tower on top was painted with the signs of the zodiac.[14] When the priest climbed the seven planetary stairs to the zodiac-tower, he was attempting to reach the heavens with magical rites.

Us . . . ourselves . . . we . . . ourselves (11:4). Observe the people's focus.

4. The first "Come, let's . . ." at Babel was uttered by the humans (11:3). What was wrong with their purposes for building the city and tower?

to "make a name [renown, honor before men] for ourselves"

_____

_____

_____

_____

to avoid being scattered over the earth (see 1:27, 9:1)

_____

_____

_____

_____

_____

to reach the heavens (to contact and manipulate astral gods so as to control nature and human events)

_____

_____

_____

_____

_____

5. What sinful attitudes, values, and fears do the people's goals indicate to you?

_____

_____

_____

_____

_____

For Further Study:
Compare the people's attitude in saying, "Come let's . . ." (11:3-4), to the attitude in James 4:13-17. How are the attitudes alike?

For Further Study:
How does Revelation 13:1-18 parallel the wrong unity of Babel?

For Thought and Discussion: Does Babel have any lesson relevant to modern efforts to unite mankind? If so, how? If not, why not?

Came down (11:5). The tower was suppose to reach to the heavens, but since the Lord had to come down to see it, it failed pathetically.

6. According to 11:6, why did God frustrate the people's attempt at united accomplishment?

_____

_____

_____

_____

7. Compare the unity of Babel (Genesis 11:3-4) to the unity "in Christ" that God planned for mankind (Ephesians 2:11-22, 4:1-16; Revelation 5:6-10, 7:9-10).

   a. What are the goals of unity in Christ, according to these references?

   _____

   _____

   _____

   _____

   _____

   _____

   b. How is unity in Christ accomplished?

   _____

   _____

   _____

   _____

   _____

   _____

84

c. Therefore, what was wrong with the unity at Babel? How would sinful man's united success in technology, astrology, magic, self-preservation, and renown have hindered God's plan to redeem the race from sin (11:4,6)?

_____

_____

_____

_____

_____

_____

_____

For Thought and Discussion: Compare man's sin and God's response in 11:9 to those in 3:1-24, 4:1-16, and 6:1-9:17. What pattern recurs? What do you learn about God?

8. Was God selfish or tyrannical in frustrating man's unity at Babel? Why or why not?

_____

_____

_____

_____

_____

_____

9. In what ways are modern people like the ones who built the tower of Babel?

_____

_____

_____

_____

_____

_____

_____

Optional Application: Does 11:1-9 suggest how you might pray for the modern world? What attitudes do we need to be delivered from?

10. a. Do the human attitudes or God's response in this story offer any warnings that you might take to heart? If so, what do you need to do or guard against?

_____

_____

_____

_____

_____

b. What steps might you take in the next few weeks to avoid or abandon the errors of Babel?

_____

_____

_____

_____

_____

Study Skill—Common Errors in Interpreting Scripture

Instead of reading a passage for what God wants to say through it, people sometimes try to find in it a message for their current lives that isn't really there. God's counsel on their present concerns may be somewhere else in the Bible, but people are impatient. Some errors such people fall into are:

1. *Allegorizing.* This involves making every person and thing in a passage a type or symbol of something else. For example, a person might make Eve stand for the emotional side of the soul, Adam represent the rational side, and so on.

2. *Selectivity.* This is building an interpretation on certain words and phrases, while

(continued on page 87)

(continued from page 86)
ignoring other phrases and "the overall sweep of the passage." For instance, a person might conclude from Genesis 11:4 that building cities is wicked in itself.

3. *False Combination.* This entails combining unconnected elements in a passage and drawing a conclusion from the combination. For instance, Noah was blameless (6:9); Noah got drunk (9:21); therefore, it is not wrong to get drunk.[15]

For Further Study:
Add 9:18-11:26 to your outline of Genesis. How does this section round off chapter 1-11? How does it introduce chapters 12-50? What does it contribute to the themes about God, man, and Israel?

Shem (11:10-26)

This passage traces the chosen line down to Abram, whose family will be the focus of the rest of Genesis and the Old Testament.

Eber (10:21,25; 11:14-17). The ancestor of the Hebrews (14:13). The name means "to pass over or through."[16] The descendants of Eber's son Joktan are listed in 10:26-29, but Peleg's descendants—the line chosen to receive God's covenant—are left for chapter 11.

Genesis so far

11. You've come to the end of primeval history and the brink of patriarchal history. If you have time, get a separate sheet of paper and briefly summarize what you've learned so far about . . .

what God intended for His creation

what happened to this creation

man's character since his fall

God's responses to man's failings

God's personality, character, nature, and attributes

12. List any questions you have about 1:1-11:26.

_____

_____

_____

_____

For the group

Warm-up. Ask, "Is it important to you to make a name for yourself? Why or why not?" To encourage honesty, you might let everyone keep his answer to himself.

Noah's sons. The main point of this story is Israel's relationship to Canaan. The lesson about ridiculing one's father is secondary, though important.

Nations descended from Noah's sons. "Sons" in this genealogy means descendants. Scholars can verify the geographical ("territories," 10:5), ethnic ("clans"), political ("nations"), and linguistic ("languages") relationships among the groups named in chapter 10. You probably won't need to spend much time discussing the historical background in this section; it is meant merely to counter those who regard this part of Genesis as fictitious. However, do ask the group what the chapter contributes to Genesis.

Babel. Some people think 11:1-9 is a myth composed to explain the origin of languages. However, archaeological evidence supports the story's details, and the story's focus is not on languages. In the context of Genesis 1-11, it is another high point of human self-centered achievement (compare 3:5, 4:17-19, 6:4) which is really a low point of human sin. As in chapters 3, 4, and 6, the message is man's sinful striving for deity and God's response to that effort. What does this repeating pattern of sinful striving, judgment, and mercy reveal about God?

Some people also think that 11:1-9 portrays a selfish, domineering God. Does it? Why did God scatter the builders? How could the worldwide religious state they were building have hindered God's choice of Abraham and preparation for Jesus?

88

Breaking routine. A lesson with few questions to discuss gives you a chance to break your routine. For instance, after sharing your experiences with application over the past few weeks, you could discuss how to approach applying Scripture (see the comments labeled "Wrap-up" on page 73). Or, you could take 15-20 minutes to evaluate how your group is going. Ask questions like, "What do you like best about what we do? What do you like least? How could we better meet the goals we set in lesson one?"

Or, you could take extra time to share requests for prayer and to pray together. You could discuss how your efforts to take to heart what you learned are going. Then you could ask God to enable each other to grow in the areas you have discussed.

You might also want to plan some extra fun time into your meeting, time just to get to know each other.

Finally, since chapters 1-11 are the first of the two main sections of Genesis, you might take a few minutes to review what you've learned about God, man, and yourselves (question 11).

1. *The NIV Study Bible,* pages 28-29.
2. Kidner, pages 103-104; *The NIV Study Bible,* page 20.
3. Kidner, pages 104.
4. Yohanan Aharoni and Michael Avi Yonah, *The MacMillan Bible Atlas,* Revised Edition (New York: MacMillan Publishing Company, 1968, 1977), page 20.
5. Packer, Tenney, and White, page 4.
6. Packer, Tenney, and White, page 5.
7. Aharoni and Avi-Yonah, page 169; Packer, Tenney, and White, page 129.
8. Donald Grey Barnhouse, *The Invisible War* (Grand Rapids, Michigan: Zondervan Corporation, 1965), page 192.
9. Packer, Tenney, and White, pages 145-146; *The NIV Study Bible,* page 21.
10. Packer, Tenney, and White, page 145.
11. *The NIV Study Bible,* page 3.
12. *The NIV Study Bible,* page 22.
13. *The NIV Study Bible,* page 23.
14. Baxter, pages 43-44.
15. Fee and Stuart, page 84.
16. Howard F. Vos, *Genesis* (Chicago: Moody Press, 1982), page 54; Kidner, page 109.

The Ancient Near East

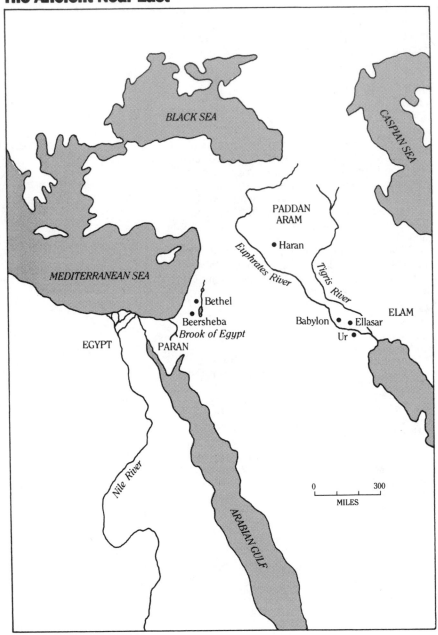

GENESIS 11:27-12:20

Abram's Call

Chapter 12 marks a turning point in Genesis. The story has been narrowing to focus on a single man, Abram, and a single line of his descendants. Having foreseen the Fall before it occurred, God had already chosen this family to fulfill His plan of redemption. The second part of Genesis traces the chosen line for four generations—from the call of Abram through the descent into Egypt.

In the next six lessons you will follow the life of Abram/Abraham, observing the man and his Lord during 175 years. If you have never read this story, it would be a good idea to read 11:27-25:11 before beginning this lesson. Otherwise, read 11:27-12:20, noticing what God and Abram do.

> ### Study Skill—Interpreting
> ### Old Testament Narratives, part three
> 6. "Narratives record what happened— not necessarily what should have happened or what ought to happen every time. Therefore, not every narrative has an individual moral of the story."
> 7. "What people do in narratives is not necessarily a good example for us. Frequently, it is just the opposite."[1]

Terah (11:27-32)

The Babel incident is centuries past, and Shem's descendants have scattered all over the Near East.

91

Some have settled in the prosperous and sophisti-
cated city of Ur on the Euphrates. Ur is a delightful
place for Semitic herdsmen until about 2180 BC,
when "hordes" of warlike "barbarians" called Guti
descend from the eastern mountains and conquer
the region around Ur. For a century, the Guti make
life miserable for the local people.[2]

In 2166 BC, about fourteen years after the Guti
invasion, a Semitic herdsman named Terah has a
son whom he calls Abram. Abram and two brothers
grow up and marry under Guti occupation. Then, at
some point, Terah decides to leave Ur for Canaan, a
thousand miles away. However, Terah stops in
Haran, four hundred miles short of his goal, perhaps
deciding that Haran is good enough. (For more on
Ur and Haran, see page 98.)

Moses calls 11:27-25:11 "the account of Terah"
(11:27), not "the account of Abram," for other
members of the family are also important. Still,
Abram remains the central human figure, overshad-
owed only by God.

To Canaan (12:1-9)

1. God gave Abram a command and a promise
   before he left Ur for Haran (Acts 7:2). What was
   the command (Genesis 12:1)?

   _____

   _____

   _____

2. The people destroyed in the Flood were noted
   chiefly as "men of renown" (6:4), and the
   people of Babel were destroyed for trying to
   "make a name for ourselves" (11:4). According
   to God's promise, how was Abram going to be
   different (12:2)?

   _____

   _____

   _____

   _____

3. What else did God promise Abram (12:2-3)?

_____

_____

_____

_____

Seventy-five (12:4). Some people think Abram
   showed lack of commitment when he stopped in
   Haran with Terah, while others think Abram
   was awaiting God's timing to leave for Canaan.

People they had acquired (12:5). "Wealthy people in
   that ancient world always had servants to help
   them with their flocks and herds. . . . Not all
   servants were slaves; many were voluntarily
   employed."[3]

4. What can we learn about Abram's character
   from his actions in 12:4-9? List the qualities
   you observe and how he shows them. (See
   Hebrews 11:8-10 for examples.)

character qualities	how Abram shows them

93

The Land of Canaan

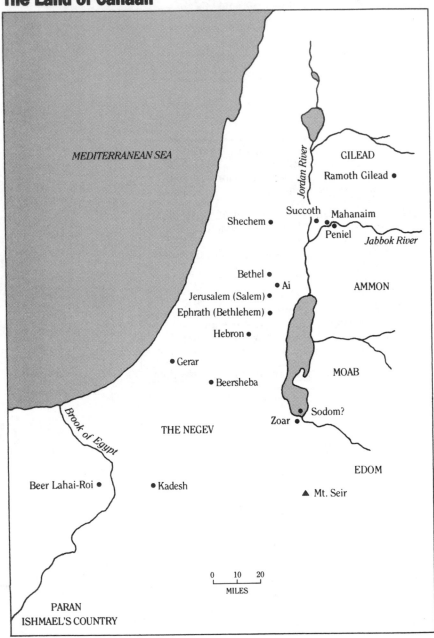

MEDITERRANEAN SEA

GILEAD

Ramoth Gilead ●

Jordan River

Succoth
Shechem ●   Mahanaim
              ●●
              Peniel   Jabbok River

Bethel ●
              ● Ai   AMMON
Jerusalem (Salem) ●
Ephrath (Bethlehem) ●

Hebron ●

● Gerar
                            MOAB
● Beersheba

                    Sodom?
Zoar ●
THE NEGEV

                            EDOM

Beer Lahai-Roi ●   ● Kadesh   ▲ Mt. Seir

Brook of Egypt

0   10   20
MILES

PARAN
ISHMAEL'S COUNTRY

Shechem . . . Bethel . . . Negev (12:6-9). See the map on page 94.

5. When Abram had obeyed God's first command, the Lord made another promise (12:7). What was it?

_____

_____

_____

_____

_____

To Egypt (12:10-20)

Egypt (12:10). Canaan depended on rainfall for fertility, so famines occurred frequently when the rains failed. Egypt's water supply from the Nile seldom failed.

Sister (12:13). Technically, Sarai was Abram's half-sister (20:12); the people of Haran favored marriage to one's half-sister. So, Abram was using "one half of the truth to conceal the other."[4]

6. What character qualities does Abram display in 12:10-13? (For instance, does he show the faith Hebrews 11:8 commends?)

_____

_____

_____

_____

_____

7. God planned to give Abram offspring through Sarai (17:15-16), but Abram almost lost her to

For Thought and Discussion: Imagine yourself as Abram. You were brought up to worship the moon, but a God named Yahweh has appeared to you. He has told you to abandon your family and their gods (both contrary to deeply ingrained tribal custom), travel to a distant country, and worship Him. How would you feel?

For Thought and Discussion: Why is it significant that the Lord gave His promises in 12:2-3,7 without conditions?

95

For Thought and Discussion: What should Sarai have said to Abram when he instructed her as in 12:11-13? The Apostle Peter commended Sarah for her submissive obedience to Abraham (1 Peter 3:3-6); is this a good example of submission? Are Peter's words in Acts 4:18-20 and 5:1-11 relevant here? Why or why not?

For Thought and Discussion: Have you ever been like Abram in 12:10-13? If so, how? How can a person avoid this error?

Pharaoh. How did God deal with this threat to His plan (12:17-20)?

_____

_____

_____

_____

_____

8. Could Abram's mistakes defeat God's plan? How is this fact significant for us?

_____

_____

_____

_____

_____

9. Did Abram's sin nullify God's promises? Why is this fact important?

_____

_____

_____

_____

_____

10. What can we learn about God from 12:1-20?

_____

_____

_____

_____

_____

_____

11. Reflect on what 12:1-20 reveals about God. What difference do these qualities make to your life?

_____

_____

_____

_____

_____

_____

_____

12. Has God given you any commands or promises? If so, how can you respond to His commands, promises, and character this week? (Does Abram offer an example to follow [12:4] or avoid [12:10-13]?)

_____

_____

_____

_____

_____

_____

_____

13. Write down any questions you have about 11:27-12:20.

_____

_____

_____

_____

_____

For the group

Warm-up. Ask everyone to think of one command or promise God has given him or her. This can be one given to all Christians or one given individually.

Read aloud.

Summarize.

Questions. To understand the extent of Abram's faith in 12:1-9, put yourselves in his place. Use the background on pages 91-92 and 98-99 to help you.

Also, try to identify with Abram in 12:10-20. Have you ever strayed from a godly path because you thought you had to take care of yourself? What does such a choice say about God? Do you need to take care of yourself?

Worship. Praise God for the qualities He exhibits in chapter 12: generosity and faithfulness, even to unfaithful people; total control of events, even when things look bleak; commitment to His plan. Thank Him for His generosity, faithfulness, control, and commitment in your lives.

From Ur to Canaan

Ur had been an important city for several thousand years before Abram was born there. It could house 34,000 people within its four square miles, behind walls 35 feet thick. But Ur's prosperity had been declining, so it was less crowded in Abram's day.

Built on a promontory between the Euphrates River and a navigable canal, Ur had two harbors that provided cheap water transportation. Donkey caravans met ships to trade gems from Russia for woods and metals from Africa; jewelry made in Ur has been found in southern India. Ur was also famous for its woolens and other goods manufactured by family craftsmen and by slaves, women, and freedmen in factories.

"The city was a marvel of architecture and design, with broad paved streets and subterranean sewage systems. The middle and upper classes lived in large, multi-storied houses with

(continued on page 99)

98

(continued from page 98)
hot and cold running water, and all enjoyed the prosperity and luxuries made possible by Ur's international commerce."[5]

Ur had a three-tiered temple-tower like the one at Babel for worshiping the moon god (called Nannar or Sin) and other astral gods. Money was lavished on the cult for music, spectacle, and sacrifice. "Religion dominated the city's activity,"[6] as well as the lives of people like Terah and Abram.

Terah probably lived outside Ur, raising sheep to supply wool for the textile weavers. He led the family to Haran, another trading center several hundred miles up the Euphrates from Ur. Haran was mostly Semitic and was also devoted to moon-worship. Again, the shepherds probably lived outside the city walls.

When Abram set out from Haran, he was leaving behind the stable water supply and city life of the Euphrates valley. He probably traveled with a caravan of other families and traders, along with flocks of sheep and goats, and five or six hundred donkeys carrying tents, blankets, food, cooking utensils, and goods to trade. The caravan drivers planned to cover fifteen miles a day, and sought a route that would allow water for the animals each night. Between Haran and Egypt, water was available only at closely guarded wells and springs, where payment had to be carefully negotiated. The Amorites who lived along the route kept track of caravans with signal fires in order to stop marauders.

Egypt, Canaan's overlord in name, kept enough peace for caravans to travel, but it did not prevent Canaanite cities from endlessly feuding over land and trade. Strangers planning to settle down were not always safe. So, Abram chose to camp in the rugged land near the semi-desert Negev. The region sufficed for grazing, if not for growing crops, and few other people used it. Abram's life included watching for lions, jackals, and bears; calling wandering sheep; separating sick animals from the herd; carrying young lambs and kids; and searching endlessly for grass and water. In a time before sheepdogs, Abram and his family and servants had to do everything.[7]

1. Fee and Stuart, page 78.
2. Eugene H. Merrill, "The Life and Times of the Patriarchs,"
   Fundamentalist Journal, volume 5, number 4 (Lynchburg,
   Virginia: Old-time Gospel Hour, April 1986), page 22.
3. *The NIV Study Bible,* page 24.
4. Kidner, page 116.
5. Merrill, page 22.
6. Merrill, page 22.
7. Harry Thomas Frank, *Discovering the Biblical World* (San
   Francisco: Harper and Row, 1975), pages 31-35; *Great People
   of the Bible and How They Lived* (New York: The Reader's
   Digest Association, 1974), pages 27,36-38.

GENESIS 13:1-15:21

Abram's Righteousness

Abram's faithlessness in Egypt could not derail
God's plan because God had a firm grasp on the situation. He got Abram and Sarai safely back to Canaan
laden with Egypt's wealth (12:16, 13:2). For a while,
at least, Abram remembered this lesson about God's
faithfulness.

Read the next episodes of Abram's life in
13:1-15:21.

> **Study Skill—Interpreting**
> **Old Testament Narratives, part four**
> 8. "Most of the characters in Old
> Testament narratives are far from perfect,
> and their actions are, too."
> 9. "We are not always told at the end of a
> narrative whether what happened was good
> or bad. We are expected to be able to judge
> that on the basis of what God has taught us
> directly elsewhere in the Scriptures."[1]

Abram and Lot part (13:1-18)

Abram first pastured his flocks in the Negev, the
semi-arid region of southern Canaan. Constantly
moving in search of fresh water and pasture, he
arrived at Bethel. There he "called on the name of
the LORD" (13:3-4)—he worshiped and prayed to the
God who had been protecting and blessing him despite his own failures.

But not even the hill country around Bethel was fertile enough to support the huge flocks Abram and Lot had acquired. Areas in the Negev and the hills were available to herdsmen only because they had too little water for settled farmers to want them. Abram and Lot soon found that if they stayed together, they could not avoid overgrazing the land and quarreling over limited water for their herds (13:6). As the senior man, Abram could have chosen the best land for himself: the plain around the Jordan River made lush by river water. However, Abram gave Lot the choice.

1. Why could Abram afford to let Lot choose the best land (12:2-3)?

_____

_____

_____

_____

2. A key phrase is repeated in 13:10,14 to contrast Lot and Abram.

   a. When Lot looked up, what did he see and choose (13:10-11,13)?

   _____

   _____

   _____

   _____

   b. What does this choice show about Lot?

   _____

   _____

   _____

   _____

   c. Abram looked up only when God commanded (13:14), and he saw the promised land—less fertile, but promised by God. Lot chose to settle in the rich cities of the plain (13:12, 19:1), but Abram chose to wander in the hills. What does this tell you about Abram? (See also Hebrews 11:9-10,13-16.)

_____

_____

_____

_____

_____

_____

Walk through (13:17). This inspection may have signified that Abram was taking title to land granted by his King.

3. a. How did God respond when Abram accepted his destiny to wander in Canaan (13:14-17)?

_____

_____

_____

_____

b. What might have been the point of this response?

_____

_____

_____

_____

_____

The Battle in Genesis 14

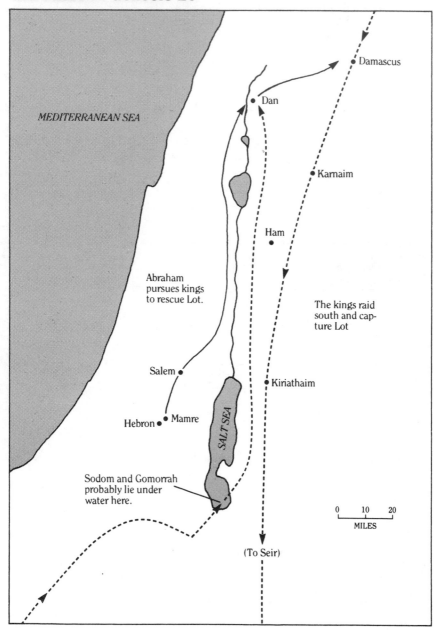

MEDITERRANEAN SEA

Damascus

Dan

Karnaim

Ham

Abraham
pursues kings
to rescue Lot.

The kings raid
south and cap-
ture Lot

Salem

Kiriathaim

SALT SEA

Hebron • Mamre

Sodom and Gomorrah
probably lie under
water here.

0   10   20
MILES

(To Seir)

Abram rescues Lot (14:1-24)

For Further Study:
How is Jesus like
Melchizedek? See
Genesis 14:18-20
and Hebrews 7:1-10.

King (14:1-2). In Mesopotamia, "sheiks" governed
individual villages and walled towns. These
sheiks were often vassals (subjects under treaty)
of "kings" who controlled wide areas. *Shinar*
was the plain between the lower Tigris and
Euphrates rivers (10:10, 11:2; see the map on
page 80). Its main city was Babylon. *Ellasar* was
a city downriver from Babylon (see the map on
page 90); *Arioch* may have ruled the villages
and towns around Ellasar as well as the city
itself. *Elam* was the region east of the Tigris.
Goiim is Hebrew for "nations" or "Gentiles,"
but a city by that name has not been found. The
overlords of Mesopotamia were aggressive in
Abram's day, and trade routes made travel for
migration or war fairly easy.[2]

By contrast, "kings" of Canaan ruled only
individual walled cities. The kings of *Sodom,
Gomorrah, Admah, Zeboiim,* and *Bela/Zoar*
were more like sheiks than kings of
Mesopotamia. Their five cities probably stood
near the Valley of Siddim in what is now the
southwest portion of the Dead Sea (14:3; see
the map on page 104). The cities were wealthy
and decadent (13:10,13; 19:1-29), great prizes
for conquerors in search of booty and tribute.

Full of tar pits (14:10). Even today, lumps of
bitumen (related to coal, asphalt, and tar) can
be found floating on the Dead Sea. The area is
also rich in petroleum, salt, sulphur, and other
minerals. The Sea itself is so salty that no life
can survive there and boats cannot pass
through.[3]

Melchizedek king of Salem (14:18). *Salem* means
"peace" and is another name for Jerusalem
(Psalm 76:2). *Melchizedek* means "king of
righteousness" (Hebrews 7:2). It was common
for the king of a Canaanite city to be the priest
of the city's cult as well.[4]

The Law of Moses established the descendants of Aaron as Israel's priests (Exodus 28:1).
When David later became king in Jerusalem, he
could not offer sacrifice as a priest because he
was not from Aaron's line. Psalm 110:1-4 proph-

105

Optional Application: How do you decide to whom to give money and with whom to make alliances? How are Abram's standards in 14:18-24 a model for you?

esied that one day a descendant of David would be both king and priest over Israel "in the order of Melchizedek," superior to the Aaronic priests. Hebrews 6:19-7:28 identifies Christ as that king-priest.

God Most High (14:18). This was a common Phoenician and Canaanite name for the chief god, but Melchizedek may have been using familiar titles to speak of the true God.[5]

Tenth (14:20). This was the share normally given to one's king (1 Samuel 8:15,17),[6] so Abram was acknowledging the authority of the king-priest of Salem.

4. Abram was selective with his alliances in 14:18-24.

a. Why did he accept Melchizedek's blessing and food and even tithe to him (14:18-20,22)? What did this gesture demonstrate?

_____

_____

_____

_____

_____

_____

b. Abram refused to accept a share of the booty, which would have indicated alliance, from the king of Sodom (14:21-24). What did this decision show about Abram (12:2, 13:13, 14:23)?

_____

_____

_____

_____

_____

106

God cuts a covenant (15:1-21)

Abram chose to resist the temptation of Sodom's riches in both chapters 13 and 14. In response, he received another vision of the Lord.

5. God told Abram not to be afraid (15:1). What was Abram tempted to be afraid of (13:14-16, 15:2-3)?

_____

_____

_____

_____

_____

6. Reflect on what the Lord said about Himself (15:1). What did each statement mean? What implications should it have had for Abram's actions?

I am your shield (12:12,17; 14:20)

_____

_____

_____

_____

_____

I am . . . your very great reward (13:12, 14:22-23)

_____

_____

_____

_____

_____

Optional Application:
a. What are you tempted to fear?
   b. Is the Lord your shield and reward? What difference does this fact make to your life?

For Thought and Discussion: How had God already acted as Abram's shield and great reward?

107

For Thought and Discussion: Is it wrong for us to ask God for reassurances of His promises (15:2-3,8)? Why or why not?

A servant . . . will be my heir (15:3). Ancient documents confirm that it was common for a childless man to adopt a servant to be his heir.[7]

7. The vision of 15:1 prompts Abram to ask why the promise of offspring (12:2, 13:16) has not yet been fulfilled (15:2-3).

a. How does God respond to Abram's question (15:4-5)?

_____

_____

_____

_____

_____

b. Was Abram's question faithless or faithful? Why do you think so?

_____

_____

_____

_____

_____

8. Why did God account Abram righteous (Genesis 15:6, Romans 4:18-22)?

_____

_____

_____

_____

_____

_____

Believed the LORD (15:6). The Apostle Paul asserted
that Abraham was an example of someone who
received righteousness by faith apart from works
(Romans 4:1-25). This interpretation of Genesis
15:6 was a challenge to the one current among
Jews of Paul's day. The Jews held that
Abraham's faith was the greatest of his many
meritorious works that earned his righteous
status before God. Rabbi Shemaiah (about 50
BC) wrote, "our father Abraham became the heir
of this and the coming world simply by the
merit of the faith with which he believed in the
LORD, as it is written: 'He believed in the
LORD, and he counted it to him for
righteousness. . . .'"[8] This was the standard
Jewish view: faith was a work that merited
righteousness. By contrast, Paul insisted that
faith was the right attitude of the ungodly that
allowed them to receive righteousness as a gift
(Romans 4:1-25).

9. a. How is Genesis 15:1-6 a model for us?

_____

_____

_____

_____

_____

_____

b. Is there any specific way in which you can
follow this example currently? If so, explain.

_____

_____

_____

_____

_____

**Optional
Application:** a. In
15:7, God identifies
Himself in terms of
His relationship to
Abram. What might
He say in your case:
"I am the LORD,
who . . ."?
    b. How should
you respond to this
Lord?

**For Thought and
Discussion:** Does
15:4-7,9-21 suggest
that God thought
Abram's questions in
15:2-3,8 were faith-
less? Why or why not?

I am the LORD, who brought you out . . . (15:7).
    "Ancient royal covenants often began with (1)
    the self-identification of the king and (2) a brief
    historical prologue, as here (see Exodus 20:2)."[9]

Covenant (15:18). The covenant in 15:9-21 resem-
    bles an ancient royal grant, like the one with
    Noah in 9:8-17 (see page 68). It is an uncondi-
    tional grant of land to Abram's descendants in
    perpetuity.
        It was common for the parties to a cove-
    nant to take an oath to abide by their promises.
    They would cut animals in half, walk down an
    aisle *between the pieces* (15:17) and invoke a
    curse: "May it be so done to me [that is, may I
    be cut in half] if I do not keep my oath and
    pledge."[10] Therefore, *made a covenant* in 15:18
    is literally "cut a covenant." (Jeremiah 34:18-19
    refers to the same ceremony.) In Genesis
    15:9-21, only God passed between the pieces;
    the land grant did not depend upon Abram
    keeping any promises.
        As strange as the rite in 15:9-21 sounds to
    modern ears, it was familiar to Abram, equiva-
    lent to signing a contract and filing it with the
    local authorities.

10. One of the key facts the Old Testament stresses
    about God is that He makes formal, legal cove-
    nants with people. What does this tell you
    about His nature?

    _____

    _____

    _____

    _____

    _____

    _____

11. Why is it important to us that God's land grant
    to Abram did not depend on his obeying any
    laws (Romans 4:13-17)?

110

_____

_____

_____

_____

_____

_____

Amorites (15:16). One of the groups inhabiting
Canaan (see Exodus 3:8). God may have been
speaking of the Canaanites in general, whose
sin was described on page 78. The name
Amorite means "westerner" in Akkadian, for the
Amorites invaded Mesopotamia and Canaan
from west of Akkadia (part of Mesopotamia).
Perhaps two centuries before Abraham was
born, the Amorites swept into Canaan and
leveled the cities there. "All lay unoccupied for
at least a couple of centuries." The cities east of
the Jordan River were not rebuilt for a thousand
years, just in time to face the Israelite invasion
under Joshua.[11] Thus, God timed the Exodus
carefully so that Israel would encounter Canaanite cities with just the right degree of strength
and sin.

---

12. God planned to postpone the fulfillment of His
promise for seven hundred years—three
hundred from the promise until Jacob entered
Egypt and four hundred more until Moses led
Israel out of Egypt (15:13).

   a. What purpose did this postponement serve for
   Abram and his descendants (Hebrews
   11:13-16,20-22)?

   _____

   _____

   _____

   _____

111

b. What other purpose did it serve (Genesis 15:16)?

_____

_____

_____

_____

_____

c. In a similar way, God is waiting to fulfill the promise of His Kingdom. Why is He waiting? (See 2 Peter 3:9, for instance.)

_____

_____

_____

_____

River of Egypt (15:18). Not the Nile, but a small river or brook in the northeastern Sinai that separates Egypt from Palestine.[12] Israel achieved borders from this river to *the Euphrates* only briefly, during David's and Solomon's reigns (1 Kings 4:20-21, 2 Chronicles 8:7-8).[13] Modern Israel is much smaller.

Summary

13. Summarize how Abram showed faithfulness to God in 13:1-15:21. (See, for instance, 13:12-18, 14:18-24, 15:1-11.)

_____

_____

_____

_____

14. How did God show faithfulness to Abram (13:14-17, 14:14-16, 15:1-21)?

_____

_____

_____

_____

_____

15. How can you follow Abram's example and respond to God's faithfulness this week? Make at least one specific plan. (Consider the optional questions in this lesson.)

_____

_____

_____

_____

_____

_____

16. List any questions you have about 13:1-15:21.

_____

_____

_____

_____

For the group

Warm-up. Ask everyone to name one way in which God has been faithful to him or her. If group members draw a blank, ask them to think of what God has promised them through the New Testament and how He has fulfilled any of those promises.

113

The point of this question is that like Abram, we have received many promises from God. Like Abram, we have seen some fulfilled but must wait to see others fulfilled. Abram depended on God's record of faithfulness day to day to sustain faith that other promises would someday be fulfilled. As you study 13:1-15:21, observe how God encourages Abram's faith along the way and how Abram responds at critical moments.

Questions. Look at each episode in 13:1-15:21 for what it reveals about Abram, God, and the covenant. Then look for lessons for your own lives.

Melchizedek (14:18) is a type of Christ; that is, he can teach us some things about Christ because he is like Christ in some respects. Hebrews 7 outlines these similarities. Although Hebrews 7:3 says he is without beginning or end in Genesis "like the Son of God," some people believe that Melchizedek *is* the Son of God in an appearance before the Incarnation. This theory raises theological problems, so you should research it beforehand if you decide to discuss it.

Summarize.

Worship. Praise God as your shield and great reward. Praise Him for the covenant He made with Abram and the way He was faithful to it. Ask Him to show you how to respond faithfully as Abram did.

1. Fee and Stuart, page 78.
2. T. G. Pinches, "Elam," *The International Standard Bible Encyclopaedia*, volume 2, pages 917-923; T. G. Pinches, "Ellasar," *The International Standard Bible Encyclopaedia*, volume 2, page 938; David Alexander and Pat Alexander, editors, *Eerdmans' Handbook to the Bible* (Grand Rapids, Michigan: William B. Eerdmans Publishing Company, 1973), page 137.
3. Kidner, pages 120, 135.
4. Packer, Tenney, and White, page 5; Kidner, page 121.
5. Kidner, pages 121-122.
6. *The NIV Study Bible*, page 27.
7. Kidner, page 123; *The NIV Study Bible*, page 28.
8. *Mekilta* on Exodus 14:31, quoted in C. E. B. Cranfield, *Romans: A Shorter Commentary* (Grand Rapids, Michigan: William B. Eerdmans Publishing Company, 1985), page 85.
9. *The NIV Study Bible*, page 28.
10. *The NIV Study Bible*, page 29.
11. Packer, Tenney, and White, page 89.
12. *The NIV Study Bible*, page 29.
13. Kidner, page 125.

GENESIS 16:1-17:27

Abram to Abraham

The covenant ceremony of 15:9-21 was impressive, but now years have passed and Sarai has no son. Abram is eighty-five years old (12:4; 16:3,16), and Sarai is seventy-five (17:17). What is God waiting for? What should Abram and Sarai do? Abram was a tower of faith in the last three chapters, but it is hard to stay that way when God seems silent and inactive. To see how Abram deals with the pressure and how God responds, read 16:1-17:27.

Hagar (16:1-16)

Sleep with my maidservant (16:2). Assyrian marriage contracts, a Babylonian law code, and other sources confirm that this was a customary way to obtain a male heir. The child of Hagar would be reckoned as Sarai's.[1]

1. It was lawful for Abram to beget an heir through Sarai's maid. However, what attitude toward God did this attempt show? (Compare 15:4-6.)

_____

_____

_____

_____

For Thought and Discussion: a. How do Abram's and Sarai's actions in 16:1-6 threaten God's plan (17:15-21)? Is the plan in serious danger? Why or why not?

b. Why are these facts important for us to remember?

Optional Application: Consider the promises God has given you. To what extent are you responsible to see that they are fulfilled? Have you ever tried to do God's job for Him? Talk to Him about this.

Optional Application: Does Abram or Sarai set any example in 16:1-6 that you need to take steps to avoid? If so, what do you need to do?

2. What character qualities did Abram display in this incident (16:1-6)?

_____

_____

_____

_____

_____

3. How did Sarai treat God and other people in . . .

16:2-3? _____

_____

_____

16:5? _____

_____

_____

16:6? _____

_____

_____

Angel of the LORD (16:7). "Angel" means "messenger." This person is distinguished from the Lord in that he is called the Lord's messenger, but he is identified with the Lord in that he speaks for God as "I" (16:10). Verse 13 says that "the LORD" spoke to Hagar. Thus, many Christians conclude that this messenger, who is both the Lord and someone sent in the Lord's name, is the Son of God appearing before His full Incarnation.[2] Other believers think the Lord's messenger speaks on His behalf, in His name, but is not the Lord.[3]

4. How does the Lord treat Hagar in 16:7-12? (What does He tell her to do? What does He promise? What does He say about Himself?)

For Thought and Discussion: a. One school of theology stresses that God is on the side of the oppressed. How does God treat the oppressed Hagar in 16:7-16? Does He do what you would expect? Why does He insist on 16:9?

_____

_____

_____

_____

_____

_____

_____

5. What does Hagar call the Lord in 16:13?

_____

_____

_____

6. Consider 16:7-13 carefully. What do these verses show about God?

_____

_____

_____

_____

_____

_____

Circumcision (17:1-27)

Thirteen years separate chapters 16 and 17. Abram is ninety-nine years old and Ishmael is thirteen (17:24-25). For all this time God has been silent, leaving Abram to tend sheep and believe that Ishmael is the promised heir. Sarai has perhaps grown used to barrenness and tolerates Hagar and her son. Now, without warning, the Lord breaks in again.

_____

God Almighty (17:1). _El Shaddai_ means "God, the Mountain One." It may suggest God's symbolic

117

For Thought and Discussion: The core of the Lord's promise is "to be your God and the God of your descendants" (17:7). What rights and promises does this imply?

For Thought and Discussion: What does it mean to "walk before me and be blameless" (17:1)?

home (Psalm 121:1), but it stresses His mountainlike might. Scripture often calls God a Rock (Deuteronomy 32:4).[4]

As in 15:7, God introduces a covenant by identifying Himself.

7. God cut His covenant with Abram in 15:9-21; now He confirms and establishes it (17:2,7).

a. What is God's side of the agreement (17:2,4-8)?

_____

_____

_____

_____

_____

b. What was Abram's only responsibility in chapter 15 (15:6)?

_____

_____

_____

_____

_____

c. What does God add to Abram's responsibility in 17:1,9-14?

_____

_____

_____

_____

8. Recall what the right to name someone represented (page 29). What was the Lord claiming

118

when He renamed Abram and Sarai (17:5,15)? (*Optional:* See Isaiah 49:1.)

_____

_____

_____

For Thought and Discussion: In what sense is God's covenant with Abraham "an everlasting covenant" (17:7)? What does this mean for our relationship to God?

Alien (17:8). Parallel words are "stranger" and "sojourner" (see 12:10, 15:13, 21:23). Tribal relationships were all-important in Abraham's day. Since there was no central government, wrongdoers were punished by relatives of the aggrieved person. An alien, who had no relatives around to protect and avenge him, was therefore vulnerable. Aliens lacked many rights of tribe members; for instance, people would seldom sell land outside the tribe (23:1-16).[5]

Circumcision (17:11). Hebrews spoke of "cutting" a covenant, and God was "cutting" a covenant in Abraham's flesh (17:13). Circumcision and obedience to God were Abraham's side of the covenant God was making with him and his descendants. God said that uncircumcised men would be "cut off" from the covenant (17:14)[6] just as circumcision cut off some of man's flesh.

9. Like the rainbow in 9:13, circumcision was "the sign of the covenant" (17:11) between Abraham and God. What central element of the covenant did circumcision signify (Genesis 15:6, 17:1; Romans 4:11)?

_____

_____

_____

_____

10. Why is it important for us that God commanded circumcision *after,* and as a sign of, faith and commitment (Romans 4:9-12)?

_____

119

Optional Application: Put yourself in Abraham's place. For thirteen years you have set your hope on Ishmael. Now everything is changing. How does Abraham react (17:17-18)? How would you react? How should you react when God suddenly changes a situation you thought was secure?

Optional Application: a. How can you show your faith in and commitment to God this week?
   b. How can you walk with God blamelessly?

11. Observe how 17:23 begins. What do you learn about Abraham that is a good example for us?

12. Since Jesus came, God no longer requires His people to be circumcised. However, what does He still require (Genesis 15:6, 17:1; Galatians 5:6)?

13. a. Is there any truth from 16:1-17:27 that you would like to apply? If so, what is it?

120

b. How do you fall short or want to grow in this area?

_____

_____

_____

_____

_____

_____

c. How can you begin to put this insight into practice this week?

_____

_____

_____

_____

_____

14. List any questions you have about 16:1-17:27.

_____

_____

_____

For the group

Warm-up. Ask everyone, "Think of a promise God has made to you that He has not yet fulfilled. How does the waiting make you feel?" The purpose here is to put yourselves in Abram's and Sarai's shoes.

Read aloud. To break up a long passage, read and discuss chapter 16, then read and discuss chapter 17.

Hagar. The main issues here are what God's treatment of Hagar tells us about Him, and how Abram's and Sarai's behavior are examples for us to avoid.

Chapter 16 shows how the ancient version of surrogate motherhood affected the family. What was wrong with the practice in general? Why was it especially wrong in light of God's plan for Abram and Sarai? Can we use this passage to condemn modern forms of surrogate motherhood, or are the circumstances not really parallel? Or, should we pay more attention to Sarai's and Abram's motives and attitudes toward God, and consider how we should or shouldn't act with similar motives and attitudes?

Notice that God promises to care for Hagar *while* she submits to domination by Sarai; He doesn't release her from the humiliating submission. However, in the Exodus God liberates Israel from slavery. Is He inconsistent not to free Hagar? Does He ever have reasons for allowing us to endure oppression as we submit to authority? Does His command that Hagar submit justify Sarai in oppressing her? If you are interested in God's attitude toward authority and submission, 16:7-16 is rich material for discussion, but be careful about the generalizations you draw from one unique event.

The identity of the angel of the Lord is still debated by scholars, and many of the best are uncertain. Consult commentaries if you are interested.

Circumcision. Discuss God's and Abraham's obligations under this next phase of the covenant. Clarify what circumcision meant; the idea of a self-cursing oath is foreign to us, but it was familiar in Abraham's time. Point out that circumcision was not a work that magically assured salvation, but rather a sign of faith and commitment. Paul criticized his fellow Jews for distorting this original meaning of circumcision. How is Christian baptism like and unlike circumcision?

Worship. Thank God for being your God, the God who hears, sees, and cares for you as He did Hagar. Thank Him for remaining faithful to you despite your failures, just as He remained so to Abraham and Sarah despite theirs. Ask Him to show you how to walk with Him and be blameless, to act out your faith in love.

1. Kidner, page 126; *The NIV Study Bible*, page 29.
2. Kidner, pages 33-34.
3. *The NIV Study Bible*, page 29.
4. *The NIV Study Bible*, page 30; Kidner, pages 128-129.
5. Roland de Vaux, *Ancient Israel: Volume 1: Social Institutions* (New York: McGraw-Hill Book Company, 1961), pages 3-12.
6. *The NIV Study Bible*, page 31.

GENESIS 18:1-19:38

God Visits

What would happen if God or His angel-messengers came to your town or your front door? When God visits, people's priorities are quickly laid bare. Read 18:1-19:38, noticing the priorities of Abraham, Sarah, Lot, Lot's family members, and the Sodomites.

Sarah laughs (18:1-15)

Men (18:2). "At least two of the 'men' were angels" (19:1), the Lord's messengers. "The third may have been the Lord himself" (18:1,13,17,20, 22,26,33).[1]

Hurried (18:2). Because a person without a tribe was vulnerable, and anyone might find it necessary to travel, hospitality was a duty and a virtue in the Near East. People often disputed for the honor of entertaining a guest, but the sheik usually won the privilege. The stranger could expect hospitality for three days, then protection in the area for a given time.[2]

Genesis 18:2-8 stresses Abraham's hospitality. Although it was "the midday siesta"[3] (18:1), Abraham hurried to serve his guests (18:2,6-7). Haste was unusual in that culture except in situations like these. Abraham ***bowed low*** (18:2) and called one of his visitors ***my lord*** and himself ***your servant*** (18:3). "He acted as if

123

it would be a favor to him if they allowed him to serve them"[4] (18:3-5). He gave them *water* to soothe hot, tired, dirty feet (18:4). He prepared a lavish meal: twenty quarts of *fine flour* (18:6) would have made a lot of good bread; people seldom ate meat at all, but a *tender calf* (18:7) was saved for special occasions; *curds and milk* (18:8) were ordinary but refreshing fare. It would have taken several hours of work to bake bread and roast a calf. Finally, Abraham *stood near* the guests like a servant while they ate (18:8).

1. Why did the Lord rebuke Sarah's laughter (18:12-14) but not Abraham's (17:17-22)? What must have been different about the spirit behind each person's laugh?

_____

_____

_____

_____

_____

2. a. What was it important for Sarah to believe (18:14)?

_____

_____

_____

_____

   b. Why was it necessary that she believe this? (*Optional:* See Hebrews 11:11 in KJV, RSV, NASB, or the NIV footnote.)

_____

_____

_____

_____

3. Does 18:1-15 teach anything about God or people that is relevant to your life? If so, jot it down.

_____

_____

_____

_____

_____

_____

_____

_____

Abraham intercedes (18:16-33)

Chosen (18:19). Literally "known"; this is often an intimate word in Hebrew. In 4:1, "lay with" is literally "knew."

4. In 18:19, the Lord describes the three-step essence of His relationship with Abraham. What are those three steps? (Notice the phrase "so that" [NIV] or "in order that" [NASB].)

a. _____

_____

_____

b. so that _____

_____

_____

c. so that _____

_____

_____

Optional Application: How is 18:19 applicable to you?

For Thought and Discussion: a. Why did God tell Abraham His plans? What do you think He wanted Abraham to do?

b. What was the point of interceding for Sodom? Did Abraham affect what God did?

5. What connection between God's grace and man's deeds do you observe in 18:19?

_____

_____

_____

_____

_____

_____

6. Because of His covenant relationship with Abraham (18:19), God decides to do something He would do with no one else. What extraordinary thing does He do (18:17,20-21)?

_____

_____

_____

_____

7. Because of his intimacy with God, Abraham dares to respond in an astonishing way. How does he respond (18:23-33)?

_____

_____

_____

_____

_____

_____

Judge (18:25). In Hebrew, this word referred to someone who was as much a leader and ruler, making and enforcing laws, as he was a person who decided legal cases. The judges in the book of Judges were often people chosen to lead a group of clans in battle.

126

8. What attitudes toward God, people, and self
   does Abraham express in 18:23-33?

**Optional
Application:** For
whom can you inter-
cede as Abraham
did?

God _____

_____

_____

_____

people _____

_____

_____

_____

self _____

_____

_____

9. Is there any example or insight in 18:16-33 that
   you would like to act on? If so, write down what
   the insight is and how you intend to apply it.

_____

_____

_____

_____

_____

_____

_____

Destruction and deliverance (19:1-38)

In the gateway (19:1). The city gate was the usual
meeting place for the local officials; the law was

**Optional
Application:** What is
the difference
between entertaining
friends and showing
hospitality to
strangers? How can
you apply Hebrews
13:2?

**For Thought and
Discussion:**
Contrast Abraham's
effect on events
(18:32, 19:29) with
Lot's inability to
influence people
(19:6-9,14,26). How
were the two men dif-
ferent? Is there a les-
son here for us?

**For Thought and
Discussion:** Observe
what has happened to
parenthood and the
status of women even
in a somewhat "right-
eous" family
(19:8,30-38). How
has this happened?
What is the solution?

discussed, decided, and administered there.
Apparently, Lot had not only rejected wandering
for city life but had even become a member of
Sodom's council of elders.[5]

10. Like 18:2-8, 19:1-8 stresses Lot's hospitality—
he takes seriously his duty to refresh and protect strangers (19:2,8) even in the face of
danger. In light of 19:4-5,9, why is it important
to emphasize Abraham's and Lot's hospitality?

_____

_____

_____

_____

_____

Moabites . . . Ammonites (19:37-38). Two nations
bordering Israel that became bitter enemies of
Abraham's descendants (Deuteronomy 23:3-6).

11. Review the progress of Lot's life since leaving
Abraham. What does he do or experience in
each of these passages? What does he show
about his faith and character?

13:12-13 _____

_____

_____

14:11-12,16 _____

_____

_____

19:1-2 _____

_____

19:8 _____

For Thought and Discussion: What moral does the fate of Lot's wife teach (**19:17,26**)? (*Optional:* See Luke **17:31-33.**)

19:15-16 _____

19:18-20 _____

19:30 _____

19:33,35 _____

12. What can we learn from the results of Lot's choices?

_____

129

_____

_____

_____

13. The ten righteous people of 18:32 shrank to
    three pathetic ones by 19:30. Why did God save
    Lot and his daughters (19:29)?

_____

_____

_____

_____

14. What has God revealed about His nature and
    values through the way He dealt with Abraham,
    Sodom, and Lot in 18:16-19:29? Write down
    what we can learn about God from this section.

_____

_____

_____

_____

_____

_____

_____

15. a. What is the most significant truth you
       learned from 18:1-19:38 about God or what
       He desires of His people?

_____

_____

_____

_____

_____

130

b. If you have not already done so in question 3 or 9, describe one step you can take to apply this truth to your life during the coming week.

_____

_____

_____

_____

_____

16. List any questions you have about 18:1-19:38.

_____

_____

_____

_____

For the group

Warm-up. Ask, "Have you ever seriously interceded with the Lord for someone or someplace other than yourself and your home? What was the situation that moved you to pray?" This question should prepare the group to think about what Abraham did for Lot and Sodom.

Read aloud.

Summarize.

Sarah laughs. Question 1 requires thoughtful inference, not wild speculation. In 17:17, does Abraham really doubt God can do what He says? Is Sarah focused on God's plans or personal pleasure? In what spirits might a person laugh—amazement, ridicule . . . ? Which kinds of laughter dishonor God, and which do not?

Question 2b makes no sense if you use the regular NIV reading. In most other versions, Hebrews 11:11 says that Sarah's faith was as necessary as Abraham's to the birth of Isaac. Commentators think it was for Sarah's sake that God repeated His promise from 17:15-21 in 18:9-15. Genesis usually focuses on the men of each generation, but the women are still important in God's plan.

Abraham intercedes. This passage raises the mysteries of intercession: How can our prayers affect what an omnipotent, omniscient, unchanging God does? Why did God want Abraham to intercede for Sodom? Would God have done anything differently if Abraham had prayed differently or not at all (notice that God saved less than ten people)? Do we have to know why intercession is necessary and effective before we do it? You probably won't come up with pat answers to any of these, but thinking about them may motivate you to pray individually and as a group. Make plans to follow Abraham's example.

Destruction and deliverance. Trace the downward spiral of Lot's life ever since he chose to settle at Sodom. What applicable lessons can we learn from his choices and their results?

Also, observe what this episode shows about God. What difference do these aspects of His nature make to you?

Summarize.

Worship. Praise God for His hatred of wickedness, His mercy on people like Lot, His faithfulness to His friends like Abraham, and His desire that His people intercede for others. Take time to intercede for your friends, relatives, neighbors, church, nation, or others in danger of God's judgment.

1. *The NIV Study Bible*, page 32.
2. de Vaux, page 10.
3. Kidner, page 131.
4. *The NIV Study Bible*, page 32.
5. *The NIV Study Bible*, page 33; Kidner, page 134.

GENESIS 20:1-21:34

Isaac At Last

God told Abram to go to Canaan; Abram obeyed, then ran frightened to Egypt. God restored Abram safe to Canaan; Abram acted faithfully for ten years, then doubted and had a son by a slavegirl. For thirteen years Abram pinned his hopes on that slave's son until God appeared, changed Abram's and Sarai's names, and announced that Sarah would bear Isaac in a year. Then God displayed His faithfulness to Abraham by letting him intercede for Sodom and by saving his nephew from the city's destruction.

 The announcement of Isaac, the prayer for Sodom, and the deliverance of Lot are only weeks or months past. Sarah may already be pregnant. Will Abraham keep faith with God? Will God remain faithful if he doesn't? Read 20:1-21:34.

Abraham and Abimelech (20:1-18)

Abimelech (20:2). This is a royal title like Pharaoh.[1] Later Philistine kings are called Abimelech in 26:1,8 and the heading of Psalm 34.

Sent for Sarah (20:2). The patriarchs lived far longer than we do, and Sarah was still a great beauty at age sixty-five (12:14). Now at ninety, however, she is desirable to Abimelech not for her looks but for the alliance she offers with her wealthy and powerful brother.[2]

Prophet (20:7). A person with whom God (or a god) is intimate; God reveals His will to the prophet and lets him influence His decisions through intercession. Pagans like Abimelech did not expect prophets to be moral because they did not expect the gods to be moral. However, the Lord intended His prophets to reflect His character.[3]

1. Knowing that God has promised an heir through Sarah within the year, what does Abraham do (20:1-2)?

_____

_____

_____

_____

_____

2. Recall 12:10-20; 15:1,6; 17:1,23; 18:10; 19:29. What does 20:1-2,9-13 tell you about Abraham?

_____

_____

_____

_____

_____

3. Observe how God responded even though this was the second time Abraham committed this sin, and even though it so closely followed the promise of Isaac (20:3-7,17-18). What does God's response tell you about His attitudes toward . . .

    His covenant? _____

_____

_____

_____

134

Abraham? _____

_____

_____

_____

Sarah? _____

_____

_____

_____

Abimelech? _____

_____

_____

_____

For Thought and Discussion: Why didn't God just abandon Abraham and choose a more honorable father for the covenant nation?

Optional Application: Have you learned the lesson about God in 12:10-20, 20:1-18, or do you still lapse like Abraham? Try to remember the last time you told a half-truth to protect yourself. If you have not already confessed it to God, do so now.

Isaac (21:1-7)

4. Isaac's name means "he laughs." Who was laughing (17:15-19, 18:9-15, 21:1-7)? Whose was the joke?

_____

_____

_____

_____

_____

5. God chose the name (17:19). What does it show about His personality?

_____

_____

_____

_____

For Further Study:
What New Testament
contrast do Sarah and
Hagar, Isaac and Ish-
mael, represent (Gala-
tians 4:21-31)?

6. How is Isaac a type of all Christians?

John 1:12-13 _____

_____

_____

_____

Galatians 4:21-31 _____

_____

_____

_____

_____

7. How should we live if we are free Isaac, not
slave Ishmael (Galatians 4:21,28-31;
5:1-6,13-26)?

_____

_____

_____

_____

_____

_____

_____

Hagar again (21:8-21)

Weaned (21:8). Babies were customarily weaned at
age two or three.[4] Therefore, Ishmael was sixteen or seventeen.

8. From God's point of view, why was it necessary
that Hagar and Ishmael leave Abraham's household (21:12)?

_____

_____

_____

_____

_____

For Thought and Discussion: a. What were Sarah's motives for sending Hagar and Ishmael away (21:9-10)? Were they the same as, or as noble as, God's motives?

b. Try to put yourself in Sarah's place. How would you have felt? What should she have done? Are you in any situation where you need to make a similar decision about how to treat people?

9. The Apostle Paul later used this story to explain why many Israelites had rejected Jesus and the company of believers. What truth about God and His chosen people do Isaac and Ishmael illustrate (Romans 9:6-9)?

_____

_____

_____

_____

_____

_____

_____

**God heard . . . has heard** (Genesis 21:17). Recall from 16:11 that _Ishmael_, the name God chose, means "God hears."

_____

10. God sovereignly excluded Ishmael and his descendants from His covenant people. However, how did God treat the people He set aside (21:12-21)?

_____

_____

_____

_____

_____

_____

137

For Thought and Discussion: What was God's ultimate goal in choosing Isaac and excluding Ishmael from the covenant (12:3)? Was God cruel to exclude Ishmael? Why or why not?

For Thought and Discussion: Recall what God promised in 15:1 and what Abimelech observes in 21:22. Has God kept His promise? How?

11. What does 21:12-21 show about God's nature?

_____

_____

_____

_____

_____

_____

Treaty at Beersheba (21:22-34)

Treaty (21:27). The same Hebrew word as "covenant" in 9:9, 15:18, 17:2. This is a treaty between equals, as opposed to one between a sovereign and a subject. Notice that it includes oaths (21:23-24,31), sacrificial animals (21:27), and a transaction of seven lambs to witness Abraham's title to the well (21:30).

12. Review how God treats Abraham and other people in 20:1-21:34 and what Isaac represents in the New Testament (questions 6, 7, and 9). What is the most significant insight you have had from these chapters?

_____

_____

_____

_____

_____

_____

13. How can you let something in this lesson affect your life? Is there some passage you want to meditate on, some action you want to take, or some change of attitude you want to pray about?

_____

_____

_____

_____

_____

_____

14. List any questions you have about this lesson.

_____

_____

_____

_____

For the group

Warm-up. Ask, "Does God show that He is *with* you? If so, how?"

Abraham and Abimelech. Once again, the lesson focuses on God and Abraham: 1) What does Abraham's behavior show about him—his attitude toward God and others? Do you ever act like Abraham in this way? What can you do about this trait? 2) What does God's response show about Him? How is this a challenge or encouragement to you?

If it seems strange that God waited for sinful Abraham to pray before healing Abimelech's household, try to think of a reason why God did this. What did Abraham and Abimelech learn?

Isaac. Some applications are: Does your life show God's sense of humor? If so, how? Are you acting like freeborn Isaac, born of God's will not man's? How could your life better display this fact about you?

Hagar again. God's rejection of Hagar and Ishmael seems unloving to some people. Point out that God didn't abandon Hagar and Ishmael to starvation or damnation; He merely excluded them from His covenant in order to show that the covenant depended on His grace and sovereign choice. His ultimate goal was to have mercy on all people through Isaac's descendant. Take a clear look at God's character in this passage, and discuss how it is relevant to your lives.

Worship. Are you seeing new aspects of God in each passage of Genesis, or the same aspects consistently shown over decades and generations? Praise God for the aspects you observe, and for the ways you see them in your own life.

1. Kidner, page 138.
2. Kidner, page 117.
3. Kidner, page 138.
4. *The NIV Study Bible*, page 36.

GENESIS 22:1-25:18

Father and Sons

God and Abraham have come a long way together. At age seventy-five Abraham left Haran, and at age one hundred he finally had Isaac. But he had seventy-five more years in which to walk with the Lord and raise the child of promise (25:7). What has twenty-five years of wandering and waiting taught Abraham? Read 22:1-25:18.

Abraham's test (22:1-24)

Abraham stayed in Philistia "for a long time" (21:34); Isaac is now a teenager or a young man.

Here I am (22:1). The proper Hebrew response of a servant (Exodus 3:4; 1 Samuel 3:4,6,8).

Moriah (22:2). The Lord told Solomon to build the Temple on Mount Moriah (2 Chronicles 3:1), and that site was forever after the only lawful place where Israel could offer sacrifices to the Lord. Another hill in the region of Moriah was later called Golgotha (Mark 15:22) or Calvary.

---

1. What was God asking Abraham to give up by sacrificing Isaac (22:2; 17:3-8,19)? (*Optional:* See Hebrews 11:17-18.)

For Thought and Discussion: Note the phrases about time in 17:23, 21:14, 22:3. What was Abraham's habit? How is this an example for us? Can you apply it to some task God has given you?

141

For Thought and Discussion: Put yourself in Abraham's place. Why would the Lord ask you to sacrifice your promised son?

For Further Study: What connection do you observe between Genesis 22:6 and John 19:17?

For Thought and Discussion: a. Isaac was old enough to resist his father's attempt to bind him, but the record says nothing of resistance (22:9). What convictions and qualities might lead a young man to allow his father to sacrifice him?
  b. How did Jesus show a similar attitude (Mark 14:36, Luke 23:46)?
  c. How is this an example for us? Can you apply it in your current circumstances?

2. Observe Abraham's words: ". . . we will come back to you" (22:5) and "God himself will provide the lamb . . ." (Genesis 22:8). What did Abraham believe (Hebrews 11:19)?

_____

_____

_____

_____

_____

3. What did Abraham's willingness to sacrifice Isaac prove (22:12)?

_____

_____

_____

_____

4. How did God respond to Abraham's willingness (22:11-18)?

_____

_____

_____

_____

_____

5. What does this episode reveal about God (22:1-2,12-18)?

_____

_____

_____

_____

_____

_____

6. According to James 2:20-24, what is one lesson we should draw from Abraham's experience?

_____

_____

_____

_____

7. How is Jesus like Isaac in this story (Genesis 22:2,9; Mark 1:11, 14:36)?

_____

_____

_____

_____

_____

8. How is God like Abraham (Genesis 22:2, John 3:16)?

_____

_____

_____

_____

_____

Optional Application: Has the Lord asked you to risk losing anything? If so, do you believe He will provide (22:8,14)?

Optional Application: a. Meditate this week on Abraham's willingness to sacrifice Isaac and Isaac's willingness to die. How can you be like them?
b. Meditate on God's willingness to sacrifice Jesus and Jesus' willingness to die. How can you respond?

9. God provided a ram in place of Isaac (Genesis 22:8,13-14). How is Jesus like that ram (John 1:29, 11:49-52)?

_____

_____

_____

_____

_____

_____

10. What observation about God, Abraham, or Isaac in 22:1-19 currently seems most significant to you?

_____

_____

_____

_____

_____

11. What difference does this truth make to your life? Is there some active application you'd like to make?

_____

_____

_____

_____

_____

_____

Sarah's death (23:1-20)

The Hittite empire in Asia Minor was as great as Egypt or Babylonia in Abraham's day. At this time, the Hittites had apparently wrested control of

144

Canaan from Egypt. (Canaan has been a disputed area throughout its history.)

Genesis 23 reflects many Hittite laws and customs. Legal business was conducted at the city gate (23:10,18). People preferred an alien (23:4) to remain landless and dependent on local good will; therefore, the Hittites flattered Abraham as a "mighty prince" (23:6) and tried to give him a tomb that they would continue to own (23:6). Abraham's strategy was to appeal to one individual's profit motive. However, he wanted to buy just the cave and part of the field (23:7-9) because if he bought the whole field, Hittite law would require him to pay taxes and social obligations to the local king.[1]

Unfortunately, Ephron knew he had the upper hand. He pretended to be generous (23:10-15), but in fact four hundred shekels was several times the going rate for a field.[2] He also made Abraham buy the whole tract and so take over the feudal duties.

Why all this detail about the purchase of Sarah's tomb? First, of all the land God granted Abraham in the royal covenant of 15:9-21, Abraham actually took title to only this one field, and he paid dearly for even this. Still, the site was going to be an important memorial for the Israelites invading Canaan after Moses' death. In the rest of Genesis, notice who else was buried at Machpelah.

12. In Abraham's culture, people thought it important to be buried with their ancestors. Yet Abraham wanted to have Sarah and himself (25:7-10) buried in Canaan rather than back in Mesopotamia. What conviction did Abraham's choice of a burial site reflect?

_____

_____

_____

_____

Rebekah (24:1-67)

My country . . . Aram Naharaim (24:4,10). "Aram of the two rivers"—the Tigris and Euphrates.[3] Aram was northern Mesopotamia.

Optional Application: Even godly men like Abraham practiced polygamy (25:1-4), although God's intention was monogamy (2:24). Do you take for granted any customs of your society that conflict with God's intentions? Pray about this.

For Further Study: How does Abraham's life reflect the effects of the Fall on marriage, work, relations between people, relations between God and man? How is 3:7-19 repeated and fulfilled?

Rebekah . . . daughter of Bethuel . . . (24:15). Genesis 22:20-24 gave us a brief update on this branch of the family in order to explain who Rebekah was (you've noticed how important family connections are in Genesis). Rebekah was Abraham's grandniece.

13. Why was it important that the child of promise marry not a Canaanite but a descendant of Seth, Eber, and Terah (9:26)?

_____

_____

_____

_____

Abraham's death (25:1-11)

Abraham left everything he owned to Isaac (25:5). As Abraham's legal firstborn, Isaac had a right to at least a double portion of the inheritance. The *gifts* (25:6) to the other sons were their shares.

14. If you have time, take a quick review of Abraham's life before going further.

a. What are the most notable characteristics he displayed during his life?

12:4, 22:9-10 _____

_____

12:10-13; 20:1-2,11-13 _____

_____

15:6, 22:8 _____

_____

15:2,8 _____

146

16:3-4 _____

17:17-18 _____

17:23, 21:14, 22:3 _____

_____

18:1-8 _____

18:23-33 _____

b. How did God treat Abraham when he was obedient and when he was faithless?

_____

_____

_____

_____

c. What is Abraham's role in the plan of God that runs through Genesis?

_____

_____

_____

_____

15. You may have already planned an application in question 11. However, if some insight from your review of Abraham's life seems relevant to your life, write it down along with any plans you have to act on it.

_____

_____

_____

_____

_____

_____

_____

Optional Application: Abraham took a huge risk in abandoning family security to be a stranger and pilgrim. How can you develop an attitude toward God that leads to trustful risktaking? How can you practice this attitude in little ways or big ones?

For Further Study: Now that you've examined the whole of Abraham's life, add 11:27-25:18 to your outline of Genesis, if you are making one. How does Abraham's life fit into the themes of Genesis? What ups and downs, crises and solutions, do you want to reflect in your outline of his life?

For Thought and Discussion: Why did God send all of Abraham's sons but Isaac away from His covenant people (25:6,18)? How was this necessary to His plan (Isaiah 60:1-22, Ephesians 2:11-22)?

The generations of Ishmael (25:12-18)

Again, the uncovenanted branches of the family are dealt with before the story focuses again on the chosen branch.

Twelve tribal rulers (25:16). Just as Abraham's grandson was going to father the twelve tribes of Israel, and as Nahor had twelve sons (22:23-24), so Ishmael fathered twelve sheiks.

Havilah to Shur (25:18). Havilah's location is disputed, but Shur is in the Sinai. The modern Arabs claim to be Ishmael's descendants.

For the group

Warm-up. Ask everyone to remember the last risk or sacrifice God asked of him or her.

Questions. Chapter 24 is a wonderful story of a faithful steward, but we've de-emphasized that aspect in order to focus the lesson on how each passage contributes to the themes of Abraham's life—his commitment to God's promises and the formation of the covenant people. Feel free to give time to other aspects if you want, but do try to save time to review Abraham's life (question 14) and discuss applications. Chapter 22 is a key episode in his life, so give it special attention. How can you become willing to do what Abraham did?

Worship. Thank God for providing a sacrifice to substitute for Isaac and for you. Praise Him for the way He remained faithful to Abraham no matter what the man did. Ask God to help you become more and more willing to entrust even your most beloved hopes and offspring to Him.

1. *The NIV Study Bible,* page 39; John J. Davis, "Archaeology: Unraveling the Truth about the Patriarchs," *Fundamentalist Journal* (April 1986), page 19.
2. Kidner, pages 145-146.
3. *The NIV Study Bible,* page 40.

GENESIS 25:19-28:9

The Generations of Isaac

"Abraham left everything he owned to Isaac"
(25:5)—his flocks, his donkeys, his slaves, and his
covenant with God. Isaac also inherited both good
and bad aspects of his father's character and passed
them on to his sons. Genesis tells us much less
about Isaac than about either his father or his sons;
we learn just enough to glimpse his character, how
God treated him, and the role he played in the birth
of the covenant people.

Read 25:19-28:9, observing the actions of God
and humans. Ask God to speak to you through this
story.

Isaac and Abimelech (26:1-33)

Before studying Isaac's family life, we'll look at his
public dealings.

1. When famine threatened Isaac, what did God
   say to him (26:1-5)?

   _____

   _____

   _____

   _____

   _____

   _____

For Thought and Discussion: Why is the basis of God's promises to Isaac (26:3,5) important to us? What is the basis of His promises to us? (*Optional:* See Galatians 3:22, Hebrews 9:15.)

Optional Application: Do you resemble your parents in any negative ways? Think and pray about this. If you decide that you do, ask God to break the influence of this kind of inheritance. Also, ask Him if there is anything you can do to change your habits.

2. On what were God's promises to Isaac based (26:3,5)? (For example, did they depend on Isaac's deeds?)

_____

_____

_____

_____

3. How did Isaac respond to God's commands and promises?

26:6 _____

_____

26:7 _____

_____

_____

4. What does Isaac's response tell you about him? (Compare 12:4,10-13; 20:1-2.)

_____

_____

_____

_____

_____

_____

The water is ours! (26:20). Sheep and goats require water every day; a large herd can drink a lot. Southern Canaan (where *Gerar* was) is low in rainfall and has almost no surface streams, so ancient herdsmen depended on wells that tapped underground streams and reservoirs. If a well gave only enough water for one group of herdsmen, rival groups often quarreled over rights. Likewise, a dispute might start if someone dug a well that tapped another well's source.

5. Despite Isaac's lack of trust, how did God continue to treat him (26:12-33)?

_____

_____

_____

_____

6. What does 26:1-33 show about God?

_____

_____

_____

_____

_____

God's choice (25:19-34)

Paddan Aram (25:20). The "plain of Aram"; the same place as Aram Naharaim in 24:10.[1]

The older will serve the younger (25:23). Ancient law required "that, under ordinary circumstances, the younger of two sons would be subservient to the older."[2]

    For most of their history, the descendants of Jacob (the Israelites) and those of Esau (the Edomites) were enemies (Numbers 20:14-21, Obadiah 9-10).

7. God told Rebekah His plan for her children (25:22-23). What was it?

_____

_____

_____

_____

For Thought and Discussion: The descendants of Esau eventually received God's grace through Jesus, a descendant of Jacob. In light of this fact, was God cruel to choose Jacob and reject Esau? Why or why not?

For Further Study: As you examine Jacob's life, keep in mind the word *tam* (quiet, cool, innocent). When does Jacob show his coolness? When is he innocent but accused, and when is he guilty?

8. According to the Apostle Paul, what does the case of Jacob and Esau reveal about God (Romans 9:10-16)?

_____

_____

_____

_____

Esau (25:25). Sounds like "hairy." His other name *Edom* (25:30) sounds like "red."[3]

Jacob (25:26). Literally, "May he be at the heels"; in other words, "May God be your rearguard [protector]." But the name could also be taken as describing a person who dogs another's steps, supplants, deceives, or betrays. In a good sense, it could name a man who holds tenaciously to his goals and duties.[4]

Quiet (25:27). "Peaceful" in NASB; "plain" in KJV. The Hebrew word *tam* suggests "sound," "solid," "level-headed," "cool."[5] Ironically, it normally means "blameless," "perfect," or "innocent" (Genesis 6:9; Job 1:1,8; 2:3.)[6]

Birthright (25:31). This included the firstborn's right to a double portion of the inheritance as well as the leadership of the family after the father's death.

Swear (25:33). "A verbal oath was all that was required to make the transaction legal."[7]

9. a. Describe Esau's character and values from the following passages:

25:27,29-34 (*Optional:* See Philippians 3:18-19, Hebrews 12:16-17.)

_____

_____

_____

152

26:34-35, 28:6-9 _____

_____

_____

_____

b. Did God or Jacob cheat Esau out of an inheritance he deserved? Why or why not?

_____

_____

_____

Isaac's blessing (27:1-40)

10. This scene depicts typical family life after the Fall. God told Rebekah His plan for her sons (25:23), and she probably told Isaac. But does anyone in the family accept God's decision gracefully? Describe how each person does wrong.

Isaac (25:23,28; 27:1-4) _____

_____

_____

_____

Rebekah (25:28; 27:5-17,42-46) _____

_____

_____

_____

Jacob (25:29-34, 27:11-27) _____

_____

_____

_____

_____

Optional Application: Have you ever been tempted to give up a gift from God for something of immediate pleasure? What desires tempt you now, if any? How does Esau's example encourage you to resist such temptations?

For Further Study: Examine the effects of the Fall on women: Sarah (12:11-15, 16:1-6, 18:9-15, 20:1-2, 21:8-10); Hagar (16:1-16, 21:8-21); Rebekah (25:28; 26:7; 27:5-17,42-46); Rachel (30:1-24; 31:14-16,19; 35:16-18); Leah (29:16-30); Dinah (34:1-31); and others. How do people treat each woman? How does each behave?

For Thought and Discussion: Do we deserve to inherit the covenant Jesus offers us (Luke 22:20)? Why or why not? Why is it crucial for us to remember this fact?

Optional Application: Do you behave in your family like any of the members of Isaac's family? Talk to God about this.

Esau (25:29-34; 27:34,38,41) _____

_____

_____

_____

11. By human law, Jacob did not deserve to inherit Isaac's blessing and God's covenant. However, did Jacob's moral virtue make him deserve it? Why or why not?

_____

_____

_____

_____

12. Why is it important for us to keep questions 9b and 11 in mind? How are these truths relevant to us? (*Optional:* See Romans 9:16, Ephesians 2:8-9.)

_____

_____

_____

_____

13. Isaac inherited his father's tendency to deceive when threatened (12:10-20, 20:1-10, 26:7-11). He also played favorites with his sons contrary to God's stated plans.

    a. What principle does Galatians 6:7 state?

    _____

    _____

    b. How did Isaac experience this with regard to deception and favoritism (27:18-40)?

    _____

154

_____

_____

_____

For Further Study:
Add 25:19-28:9 to
your outline of
Genesis.

14. What lessons for our lives does 25:19-28:9 teach about God's justice, mercy, sovereignty, or unearned grace?

_____

_____

_____

_____

_____

_____

_____

15. What one truth from 25:19-28:9 would you like to apply to your life?

_____

_____

_____

_____

16. Describe any practical steps (including prayer and action) you can take to impress this truth on your heart and put it into practice.

_____

_____

_____

_____

_____

For the group

Warm-up. Ask everyone to think of one trait that he or she shares with his or her parents.

Read aloud and summarize.

Isaac and Abimelech. The issues here are how Isaac treated God and other people and how God treated Isaac. What do you learn about God and His covenant, and about families? Does God treat you as He did Isaac? Why?

You may want to deal with chapter 26 briefly, since it repeats lessons you learned from Abraham's life. However, it does give you a chance to discuss how you applied what you learned from earlier chapters about God's faithfulness despite Abraham's deeds. What have been the results of your applications?

God's choice. Paul builds a crucial piece of reasoning in his letter to the Romans around the case of Jacob and Esau. God's tendency to choose younger sons is a pattern in Genesis. What does it show about Him? Why doesn't He base His choices on human custom or virtue? What does He base them on? Why did He choose you?

Isaac's blessing. Notice how God accomplishes His plan despite the sin of the people in this family. Observe that while Isaac received much mercy and undeserved faithfulness in chapter 26, he receives justice (question 13) in chapter 27. Watch for this pattern of mercy and justice in the lives of Jacob and his sons.

Worship. Praise God for caring for His chosen ones, sovereignly carrying out His plans, and treating each person with justice or mercy. Thank Him for the way He treats you.

1. *The NIV Study Bible,* page 43.
2. *The NIV Study Bible,* page 43.
3. Kidner, page 151.
4. Kidner, page 152.
5. Kidner, pages 151-152.
6. Carl D. Evans, "The Patriarch Jacob—An 'Innocent Man,'" *Bible Review* (Washington, D. C.: Biblical Archaeology Society, Spring 1986) page 32.
7. *The NIV Study Bible,* page 44.

GENESIS 28:10-31:55

Jacob's Journey

*"In the womb he grasped his brother's heel;
as a man he struggled with God."*
Hosea 12:3

One of the great puzzles of Scripture is why God
favors some people and not others with an intimate
relationship with Himself. One of the great marvels
is how that favor affects the character of the person
in question. Jacob, the next link in the chain of
God's plan, lived both the puzzle and the marvel as
an example for us.

1. If you've never read Jacob's story, consider reading all of 28:10-35:29. If you have read it before
   or if your time is limited, read at least 28:10-
   31:55. As you do so, write a title that expresses
   what each episode is about.

   28:10-22 _____

   _____

   29:1-14 _____

   _____

   29:15-30 _____

   _____

   30:1-24 _____

   _____

For Further Study:
What did Jesus mean
in John 1:51? How is
He like the stairway
between heaven and
earth that Jacob saw?
(See John 14:6,
1 Timothy 2:5.)

30:25-43 _____

_____

31:1-21 _____

_____

31:22-55 _____

_____

Dream at Bethel (28:10-22)

Beersheba . . . Haran . . . Bethel (28:10,19). Find
these places on the maps on pages 90 and 94.
There were about five hundred miles between
Beersheba and Haran. In those days, a person
was a fool to travel without a caravan of food,
water, and companions to discourage robbers.
Jacob had neither map nor guide for the jour-
ney. *Bethel* means "house of God."

Stairway (28:12). "Ladder" in KJV, RSV. "Not a
ladder with rungs, it was more likely a stairway
such as mounted the sloping side of a ziggurat"[1] (a temple-tower like the one at Babel). A
ziggurat would have had plenty of room for
angels of God to ascend and descend. Unlike
the Mesopotamian ziggurats, however, the one
Jacob saw really was *the gate of heaven* (28:17;
compare 11:4 and the note on page 82).
Jesus said that His disciple would "see
heaven open, and the angels of God ascending
and descending on the Son of Man" (John
1:51), just as the angels did on the stairway
Jacob saw.

I will not leave you (28:15). Pagans believed that
each god had power only in a particular locality,
but the Lord promised to protect Jacob whether
in Canaan or Aram.[2]

2. Briefly list the promises God made to Jacob at
Bethel (28:13-15).

158

_____

_____

_____

_____

_____

_____

3. Jacob was beginning to know God as his fathers had known Him. What did he do in response to what he had learned (28:18-22)?

_____

_____

_____

_____

_____

_____

For Thought and Discussion: Some people think Jacob's response to God (28:18-22) shows great faith and commitment, while others think it reflects a distorted view of God. What do you think, and why?

For Thought and Discussion: Should Christians make vows to God like the one Jacob made? Why or why not?

Pillar (28:18). Ancient people often set up stone memorials "of worship or of communion between man and God."[3]

---

4. What attitudes and beliefs about the Lord do Jacob's words and actions (28:16-22) show?

_____

_____

_____

_____

_____

In Paddan Aram (29:1-31:55)

Tenth (28:22). The traditional king's share, and therefore God's share (14:20).[4]

159

For Thought and Discussion: Why do you think Moses and/or God makes such a point of the puns in the story of Jacob—Edom-red, Laban-poplar-white, Rachels and Leahs-ewes and rams, firstborn-firstborn, etc.?

Rachel (29:11). Her name means "ewe," a female sheep.[5]

Leah (29:16). This name means "cow"[6] and sounds like "ram."[7] The herdsman Laban named his daughters appropriately, but the Genesis narrative later plays on their names to make a point.

Older one (29:26). Literally, "firstborn" (KJV, NASB).

5. Jacob deceived his father by pretending to be his brother in order to usurp the right of the firstborn (27:19). How was Jacob paid back (29:21-26)?

_____

_____

_____

_____

Poplar . . . white (30:37). Jacob tried "to get the best of Laban (whose name means 'white') by means of white branches." The Hebrew for "poplar" also sounds like *Laban*.[8] In the same way, Jacob the heel-grasper got the best of his brother Edom ("red") with red stew (25:30).

Ancient people believed that "a vivid sight during pregnancy or conception would leave its mark on the embryo," although modern doctors disagree. Jacob may have thought he was double-crossing Laban with magic, but in fact only God's miraculous intervention enabled Jacob to triumph over Laban.[9]

6. In 29:16-27, Laban deceived Jacob with regard to Rachel (ewe) and Leah (cow, ram). Then he removed all the multi-colored animals from his flocks to cheat Jacob of sheep and goats (30:35-36). How did God pay Laban back for these deceptions (30:29-43)?

_____

_____

_____

_____

7. What other successful and attempted cheatings and deceptions went on in this family?

31:6-9 _____

_____

_____

31:19,32-35 _____

_____

_____

31:20,26-28 _____

_____

_____

8. Deception seems to have run in this family. Do particular sinful habits run in many families? What evidence can you offer to support your view?

_____

_____

_____

_____

_____

9. Consider what happened to each deceiver. How was each person fundamentally deceived with regard to sin and consequences (Galatians 6:7-8)?

_____

_____

_____

Optional Application: Do you practice deception or any other sin in your family? What have been the results? If you are convicted of guilt, ask God to cleanse you and your family from your sinful habit.

For Thought and Discussion: God chose this family to be His special people. Did they deserve it? Why did God choose such a flawed group? What does His choice tell you about Him?

Optional Application: Are you reaping what you have sown? Talk to God about this. If you are, what does 1 John 1:8-10 say you should do?

For Thought and Discussion: What does the Lord's response to Leah's misery (29:31) tell you about Him? What acts of kindness has He done for you?

For Thought and Discussion: Jacob and Rachel both tried to use magic to obtain fertility (30:14-15,37-43).
a. What was the real source of this blessing (30:2,22; 31:9)?
b. What attitude toward God did the use of magic show?
c. Can a modern person use magic or science with the same attitude? If so, how?

For Further Study: Observe the effects of human sin on the four women in this story: Leah, Rachel, Bilhah, and Zilpah. Notice how they are treated and how they treat others. What can Christian families do to restore the relationships God desires (such as Genesis 2:18-25 and John 15:12-13)?

_____

_____

Bridal week (29:27). It was customary to hold a wedding feast for seven days (Judges 14:10,12).

Mandrakes (30:14). The roots of this plant "resemble the lower part of a human body and were therefore superstitiously thought to induce pregnancy when eaten."[10]

Disgrace (30:23). In that culture, women were valued chiefly as bearers of sons. Barrenness was a failure to fulfill one's most valuable function.

10. a. Briefly summarize the trials Jacob went through while he lived with his uncle Laban.

   29:21-27 _____

   _____

   _____

   30:1,16 _____

   _____

   _____

   30:34-36, 31:5-7 _____

   _____

   _____

   b. With what character traits did Jacob respond to these trials?

   29:20,30 _____

   _____

   _____

   30:2,4,16 _____

162

_____

_____

30:31-33,37-43 _____

_____

_____

31:20 _____

_____

31:38-42 _____

_____

11. a. Yet, in the midst of his trials and despite his moral flaws, what did Jacob learn about God (30:30; 31:3,7,11-13)?

_____

_____

_____

_____

b. How did he respond to God (31:17-18)?

_____

_____

_____

_____

12. Take a few minutes to review what each person did in 28:10-31:55 and also what God did. Is there some insight from these chapters that seems to apply to your life? If so, write it down.

_____

_____

_____

_____

For Further Study: The twelve tribes of Israel descended from Jacob's twelve sons. Study the meaning of each son's name. Be alert for what the rest of Genesis says about each man. You could look up each name in a concordance (see page 213) to find other scriptures that refer to that tribe.

For Further Study: Look for these New Testament principles in Jacob's life: Luke 6:38, Romans 5:3-5, James 1:2-3. Do they function similarly in your life? If so, how should they affect the way you deal with situations?

For Thought and Discussion: How did God use Laban's cheating to train Jacob in godliness?

Optional Application: How are you like Jacob and how are you different?

13. How can you respond to this insight with prayer or action?

_____

_____

_____

_____

For the group

Warm-up. Ask group members to recall relationships in their own families—brothers, sisters, parents, children, in-laws. As you study Jacob's family, compare your own family relationships to Jacob's.

In Paddan Aram. You can answer question 8 from your own experience or from Scripture. Are the deceptions in Jacob's family just coincidence? Is it coincidental that King David and his sons all struggled with lust? Alcoholism, wife and child abuse, gambling, theft, temperament and adultery are all known to run in families. However, this doesn't mean that every sinful trait is inherited, nor that one is doomed to inherit family traits. Also, a person can be freed from a family sin as from any sin—by confessing, repenting, and seeking the cleansing of Jesus.

Worship. Praise God for the way He shaped Jacob with a combination of mercy and his own medicine. Praise Him for being with Jacob through all the years of his toil. Thank Him for being with and shaping you.

1. *The NIV Study Bible*, page 48.
2. *The NIV Study Bible*, page 48.
3. *The NIV Study Bible*, page 48.
4. *The NIV Study Bible*, page 49.
5. Richard Elliott Friedman, "Deception for Deception," *Bible Review* (Spring 1986), page 27; *The NIV Study Bible*, page 49.
6. *The NIV Study Bible*, page 49.
7. Friedman, page 27.
8. *The NIV Study Bible*, pages 51-52.
9. Kidner, page 163.
10. *The NIV Study Bible*, pages 50-51.

LESSON SIXTEEN

GENESIS 32:1-36:43

Israel

God told Jacob to leave Haran and return to Canaan
(31:10-13). On the way to Bethel, Jacob made some
necessary and unnecessary stops at Mizpah
(31:22-55), Mahanaim and Peniel (32:1-32), and
Shechem (33:18-34:31).

Jacob had experienced a lot during twenty
years (31:38) with Laban. He left Canaan a young
man with nothing but a strong body and a clever,
tenacious, unscrupulous character. He returned
with two wives, two concubines, twelve children,
and probably several dozen servants to manage his
large flocks and herds. Was he different in other
ways than wealth?

1. Read 32:1-35:29 and skim 36:1-43. Give a title
   to each section that summarizes what happens.

   32:1-21 _____

   _____

   32:22-32 _____

   _____

   33:1-20 _____

   _____

   34:1-31 _____

   _____

165

35:1-15 _____

_____

35:16-29 _____

_____

36:1-43 _____

_____

2. Describe the character traits and beliefs about God you observe in Jacob as he returned from Haran to Beersheba.

31:25-32 _____

_____

_____

31:36-42 _____

_____

_____

32:1-2 _____

_____

_____

32:3-8 _____

_____

_____

32:9-12 _____

_____

_____

_____

32:13-21 _____

_____

_____

Wrestling with God (32:22-32)

Optional Application: In what ways do you wrestle against God or about God? What kinds of wrestling are good, what kinds are bad, and why? Does Jacob's life illustrate any decisions you need to make regarding your wrestling?

Jabbok (32:22). See the map on page 94. Once again, God uses a wordplay to make a point. "God wrestled (*ye'abeq*) with Jacob (*ya'aqob*) by the Jabbok (*yabboq*)."[1]

Name (32:27,29). Since the ancients believed that a person's name revealed his character, telling one's name was an intimate self-disclosure. Knowing someone's name gave one a psychological advantage over that person.[2]

Israel (32:28) This would normally mean "May God strive (for him)," so the name may indicate that from now on God will strive for Jacob. Alternatively, it describes a man who struggles and perseveres against God or to know God.[3]

3. On the eve of a dreaded meeting with his brother, Jacob had another strange experience with God (32:22-32).

   a. Jacob's name means "heel-grasper," "deceiver," "supplanter," and "one who holds on tenaciously despite adversity." How had the heel-grasper struggled with men and overcome (32:28)? (Consider 25:19-32:21.)

   _____

   _____

   _____

   _____

   _____

   _____

   b. How had he also been Israel, a man who struggled with God (27:35; 28:16-22; 30:37-43; 31:3,10-13,20-21; 32:9-21)?

   _____

   _____

167

For Thought and Discussion: What does God's willingness to wrestle with Jacob tell you about Him? Is He also willing to wrestle with us? If so, how? If not, why not?

Optional Application: God transformed Jacob's heel grasping into tenacious faith, and used his wrestling to produce endurance. How could He transform your flaws into strengths?

For Thought and Discussion: What did Jacob learn about blessing in Aram (27:35, 31:5, 32:26, 33:11)?

Optional Application: On what do you rely to attain blessings? Do your actions and choices reflect your inner convictions about this?

4. Remember from page 29 what the right to name someone signified. What was God doing by changing Jacob's name to Israel (32:28)?

_____

_____

_____

_____

5. A man's name expressed his identity. What change in character did the name change from heel-grasper to God-wrestler represent?

_____

_____

_____

Confrontation with Esau (33:1-20)

Present (33:11). The same Hebrew word as "blessing" in 27:35.[4] Jacob stole Esau's blessing, but now he returns one, a tiny part of the blessing God gave him freely.

Seir . . . Succoth (33:14,17). See the map on page 94. Seir was far south of Canaan, and Jacob had no intention of going there.

6. Examine the way Jacob-Israel treats Esau in 33:1-17. In what ways does he act like the old deceiver Jacob, and in what ways do you see growth in him?

168

_____

_____

_____

_____

_____

_____

7. a. How did God keep the promise in 28:15
during the rest of Jacob's life?

30:27-31:9 _____

_____

_____

_____

31:22-35 _____

_____

_____

_____

32:6-12, 33:1-4 _____

_____

_____

33:18 _____

_____

_____

_____

b. What can we conclude about God from these
events?

_____

_____

For Thought and Discussion: How did God make sure that Jacob didn't marry a Canaanite but did eventually return to Canaan and live away from Canaanite cities (27:41-28:6, 31:1-3, 34:30)? What does the way things worked out show about God?

Optional Application: Do you have any unfinished business with another person that you should settle before going to worship God (Matthew 5:23-24)?

169

Optional Application: What moral values does each group in 34:1-31 display? Search your heart to see if you ever think or act with similar attitudes.

For Thought and Discussion: Why is it significant that "Jacob's sons replied deceitfully" (34:13)?

Detour to Shechem (34:1-31)

After crossing the Jordan River into Canaan, Jacob went north to Shechem instead of south to the more isolated Bethel. Camping near Shechem gave the clan of Israel the benefits of trade and social exchange with the prosperous Canaanites. Jacob apparently hoped to settle down there, for he bought land (33:19). However, events forced Israel back to wandering far from Canaan's cities.

Notice that chapter 33 ends with God's name and chapter 35 begins with it, but it is absent from chapter 34.

Shechem (34:2). The prince was probably named after the town.

8. The Shechemites wanted to intermarry with Israel to absorb the clan and its wealth (34:9,21-23). Why did God not want this intermarriage and alliance? (*Optional:* In Deuteronomy 7:3-4,6, see God's words to the Israelites entering Canaan.)

9. The Shechemites behaved like typical Canaanites, lustful and greedy (34:2,23). However, with what character qualities did the sons of Israel respond (34:13-17,25-31)?

170

10. What point does this detour to Shechem serve in the story of Jacob's return from Aram? Consider what happens before (32:22-33:18) and after (35:1-15). What lessons can the detour teach us in our own journeys?

_____

_____

_____

_____

_____

_____

For Thought and Discussion: a. Find Succoth (33:17) and Shechem (33:18) on the map on page 94, and compare God's command in 31:13 to what Jacob did in 33:18-19. What do you suppose he was doing in Shechem? How did this detour differ from the detour to Edom?

b. Have you ever chosen to detour to "Shechem" instead of going directly to "Bethel"? Why is this a tempting thing to do?

Return to Bethel (35:1-15)

Rings (35:4). "Worn as amulets or charms; a pagan religious custom (compare Hosea 2:13)."[5]

11. After a disastrous experience in Shechem, Jacob did two things. What were they?

35:2,4 _____

_____

_____

35:1,3,6-7 _____

_____

_____

12. What do these actions tell you about Jacob?

_____

_____

_____

_____

_____

171

For Thought and
Discussion: Why did
God confirm Jacob's
new name after he
renounced idolatry
and returned to
Bethel (35:10)?

Optional
Application: a. Why
was abandoning for-
eign gods (35:2) an
important part of
Jacob's growth as the
heir of the covenant?
b. Are any false
gods coming between
you and the true God?
If so, what can you do
about this problem?

For Thought and
Discussion: Sum-
marize how you have
seen Jacob change.
For instance, how has
he shown bad and
good traits of a
"Jacob" and an
"Israel" personality?
How have his experi-
ences with God
affected him?

13. God responded in 35:9-13.

    a. Why did He repeat to Israel the command/
    blessing He gave Adam and Noah (1:28;
    9:1,7; 35:11)? What did this repetition
    signify?

    _____

    _____

    _____

    _____

    _____

    b. Why did He repeat His promises to Abraham
    and Isaac about heirs and land?

    _____

    _____

    _____

    _____

    _____

14. Jacob lived almost to the end of Genesis, and
    God continued to shape him. Still, what have
    you learned from Jacob's example about how a
    disciple grows?

    _____

    _____

    _____

    _____

    _____

15. What one lesson from Jacob's life could you
    apply to your own walk with God?

    _____

    _____

    _____

16. How can you apply this lesson? For example, is there any prayer or action that you can pursue?

_____

_____

_____

_____

_____

Optional Application: Choose one truth Jacob learned about God, discipleship, or godly character. Write it down. Then take time at least twice during the next week to reread the relevant passages and reflect on how this truth applies to you. Thank God for this truth, and ask Him to let it take root in your life.

Rachel and Isaac die (35:16-29)

Difficulty in childbirth (35:17). Rachel used her childbearing cycle to deceive Laban and Jacob about the household gods (31:35), and she died in childbirth. Jacob had promised Laban that the person who proved to have stolen the idols would die (31:32). Some people see a connection between Rachel's sin and her death.[6]

Reuben (35:22). The firstborn would have inherited his father's concubines after his death; Reuben was acting as though his father was dead. For this offense, the rights and respect of the firstborn passed to Judah (Genesis 49:3-4,10; 1 Chronicles 5:1).[7]

The generations of Esau (36:1-43)

Esau and Edom (36:1) were names for the same person; Edom and Seir (36:9) were names for the same place. This record of the original Horite chiefs of Seir (36:20-30) and the Edomite chiefs and kings who displaced the Horites (36:9-19,31-43) takes care of Esau's line before the story again focuses on Jacob's. It was important for the Israelites entering Canaan after Moses' death to know that they and the Edomites were kin; this fact affected relations between Israel and Edom for centuries.

17. List any questions you have about the life of Jacob and what it means to you.

_____

_____

_____

For the group

Warm-up. Ask, "Would anyone like to share how he or she has grown to know God better during the last few weeks?" You may have found yourselves growing closer to God since you've been looking at His character in Genesis.

Questions. The strange scene at Peniel reveals the theme of Jacob's life: he has been a struggler against God and man. It's easy to see how he struggled with Esau, Isaac, and Laban, but perhaps less easy to see how he struggled with God. Jacob may not seem to deal with God at all except at Bethel, in the one vision in Aram, and at Peniel. However, how was Jacob's whole life really a struggle with God to see who was in control? Use the references in question 3b to jog the group's memories about Jacob's exploits.

It may also seem strange that the other wrestler in 32:22-32 says that Jacob has struggled with God *and overcome.* Notice how it is ambiguous who is the victor in the wrestling match at Peniel. Who or what did Jacob overcome in his struggle with God? In what sense was he victorious, and in what sense was God victorious?

Worship. Thank God for the ways He uses your circumstances to mature you in knowing and obeying Him. Thank Him for the specific things you are learning about Him. Ask Him to help you live by what you've learned from Jacob.

1. *The NIV Study Bible,* page 56.
2. Kidner, page 170.
3. Kidner, page 170; Barnhouse, page 125.
4. *The NIV Study Bible,* page 57.
5. *The NIV Study Bible,* page 58.
6. Friedman, pages 27-28.
7. *The NIV Study Bible,* page 59.

GENESIS 37:1-50:26

Joseph: God in Control

The story of Joseph reads like a tale told around campfires from generation to generation, a superbly crafted drama of suspense, humor, secret identities, and remarkable reversals. To the ancient Israelites, it was a high point in their family history. But beyond all this, it is an episode in *God's* story, the next stage in His sovereign plan. Although it is tempting to see Joseph as the story's hero, the narrative makes it clear that at every turn it is God who works the decisive acts.

Read straight through 37:1-50:26 before turning to the questions in this lesson. Chapter 38 is a digression with its own separate importance, and chapter 49 is a series of blessings. The rest is a classic tale you should enjoy for its own sake, while you look for the main point of the whole story. Choose a time when you can relax and take pleasure in it.

This story covers about a century in which God and people are actively fulfilling God's plans, whether the people know it or not. It's important to study a tightly unified narrative like this one as a unit, so lessons seventeen and eighteen both deal with the whole story instead of breaking it in two. For this lesson, go back through 37:1-50:26 and record your observations on these three questions:

    a. What does *God do* in this episode?

    b. What does *God allow to happen* to Joseph and other people?

    c. What *character qualities* does each person show in this episode?

In lesson eighteen you'll use these observations

to draw conclusions about how God shapes history and individual people's characters, and how Joseph and his family set good and bad examples for us. However, if you come across an insight for application as you work through questions 1-13 of this lesson, jot your thoughts in questions 14 and 15.

Dream (37:5). Dream interpretation was popular in the ancient world; the Egyptians raised it to an art. Various schools of Egyptian wise men took pride in their various systems for interpreting the voices of the gods in dreams.[1]

   The Lord did use dreams to speak to Abraham, Jacob, Abimelech, Joseph, and other biblical people. But in only two cases did He send dreams that required wise interpreters to unravel them. In both cases He was dealing with pagan cultures fascinated with dreams: Babylon in the case of Daniel, and Egypt in the case of Joseph. Both Daniel and Joseph were careful to attribute their discernment to revelations from God, never to their own wisdom.

Mother (37:10). Rachel is dead (35:16-20); this is probably Leah.

Dothan (37:17). A city thirteen miles north of Shechem.

---

1. a. What does God allow to happen in 37:1-36?

_____

_____

_____

_____

_____

_____

_____

   b. What character qualities does each person show in this chapter?

Jacob-Israel (37:3,10-11,33-35) _____

_____

_____

_____

_____

Joseph (37:2,5-11) _____

_____

_____

_____

_____

Reuben (37:21-22,29-32) _____

_____

_____

_____

Judah (37:26-27) _____

_____

_____

_____

_____

all the brothers (37:4,8,11,19-20,23-28,31-35)

_____

_____

_____

_____

_____

_____

For Thought and Discussion: Notice that in 37:21-22, 26-32 Reuben tries to act as the firstborn, responsible for Joseph and leader of the brothers. However, real leadership has passed to Judah because of Reuben's sin (35:22). Watch for Reuben's and Judah's roles in later chapters.

For Thought and Discussion: Contrast Judah's conduct in chapter 38 with Joseph's in 39.

Optional Application: How might the way God repeatedly cared for Joseph while he suffered encourage you in your present situation?

2. How does Judah behave in 38:1-30?

_____

_____

_____

_____

Captain of the guard (37:36, 39:1). Probably the head of the royal executioners, in charge of the royal prisoners.[2]

3. a. What does God allow to happen to Joseph in 39:1-23?

_____

_____

_____

_____

_____

_____

b. What does God do in these situations (39:2-6,21-23)?

_____

_____

_____

_____

_____

c. What character traits does Joseph show in this chapter?

_____

_____

_____

_____

_____

_____

_____

Cupbearer (40:1). This trusted official chose and tasted the king's wine to assure that it was not poisoned. Because he was present with the king at each meal, he had intimate access and often freedom to speak.[3]

Baker (40:1). He was less important than the cupbearer, but still had a huge charge. Some Egyptian documents list dozens of kinds of breads and pastries made daily in the royal bakery.[4]

4. a. What does God do and allow to happen in 40:1-23?

_____

_____

_____

_____

_____

_____

b. What attitudes toward his fellow prisoners and God does Joseph display (40:6-8)?

_____

_____

_____

For Further Study:
Look up *seal* and *sealed* in a concordance to see how New Testament writers use the seal as a metaphor.

Shaved (41:14). Hebrews wore beards, but Egyptians were clean-shaven.[5]

In charge of my palace (41:40). "Master of the palace" was the proper Egyptian title for the person in charge of the royal estate and revenues. But in effect, Joseph also served as First Minister of Egypt. (In Hebrew, the same term served for both functions.)

The First Minister reported each morning to the Pharaoh for instructions. "All the affairs of the land passed through his hands, all important documents received his seal, all the officials were under his orders. He really governed in the Pharaoh's name and acted for him in his absence."[6]

Signet ring (41:42). The seal or signet was a sign of authority. A man stamped his seal in wax to authorize a document or claim ownership of an object. He gave his seal to a messenger or proxy to show that the sent one carried his authority. He loaned his seal to someone to guarantee future payment.

Pharaoh wore his signet as a finger ring, while Judah wore his on a cord around his neck (38:18-19). Archaeologists have excavated both types of seals.[7]

All the world (41:57). "The known world from the writer's perspective (the Middle East)." As in the days of Noah, God chose one man through whom to deliver the world from disaster.[8]

5. a. What does God do and allow in 41:1-57?

180

_____

_____

_____

_____

_____

b. What qualities does Joseph display
   (41:16,25-36,48-57)?

_____

_____

_____

_____

_____

_____

6. a. Describe the character qualities of the people in
      42:1-38.

   Jacob (42:1-5,36-38) _____

   _____

   _____

   _____

   _____

   Joseph (42:6-26) _____

   _____

   _____

   _____

   _____

Joseph's brothers (42:6-38) _____

_____

_____

_____

_____

_____

b. What hand did God have in all this?

_____

_____

_____

_____

_____

_____

Egyptians could not eat with Hebrews (43:32).
"The taboo was probably based on ritual or religious reasons . . . unlike the Egyptian refusal to associate with shepherds (see 46:34), which was probably based on social custom."[9]

7. Describe each man's character and feelings from what he does in 43:1-34.

Jacob (43:1-14) _____

_____

_____

_____

Judah (43:3-10) _____

_____

182

_____

_____

_____

Joseph (43:15-34) _____

_____

_____

_____

8. a. What qualities do Joseph and his brothers
show in 44:1-45:15?

Joseph (44:1-5,14-15; 45:1-15) _____

_____

_____

_____

_____

_____

_____

all the brothers (44:7-13) _____

_____

_____

_____

_____

Judah (44:18-34) _____

_____

_____

_____

_____

b. What does 45:5-11 say about God's hand in the events?

_____

_____

_____

_____

_____

9. a. What does God say and accomplish in 45:16-47:12?

_____

_____

_____

_____

_____

b. What is Joseph's role in these events?

_____

_____

_____

_____

_____

c. Describe Jacob's personality in 46:1-7,30; 47:7-10.

_____

_____

_____

_____

_____

10. What did Joseph do for Egypt during his career (47:13-26)?

_____

_____

_____

_____

_____

_____

Mine, just as Reuben and Simeon are mine (48:5). Ephraim and Manasseh would enjoy equal status with Jacob's first two sons. Thus, Joseph inherits a double share of Jacob's estate as the firstborn should have, for Reuben forfeited his right (35:22). When Ephraim and Manasseh became reckoned as two tribes, the total number came to thirteen, but God planned to set Levi aside as the priestly tribe and divide the promised land into twelve allotments.

11. What important decisions does Jacob-Israel make in the following passages:

47:28-31, 49:29-32 _____

_____

_____

48:1-6 _____

_____

_____

_____

48:17-20 _____

_____

_____

For Further Study:
See Numbers 2 for
Israel's twelve march-
ing divisions and
Joshua 13-21 or a
Bible atlas for the di-
visions of the land.

**For Thought and
Discussion:** Why do
you suppose Hebrews
11:21 chooses
Jacob's act in Genesis
48 as the supreme
example of faith from
Jacob's life?

**For Thought and
Discussion:** How is
Joseph's desire in
Genesis 50:24-26 a
model for Christians?
See Hebrews 11:22.

What will happen to you (49:1). The blessings in
49:2-27 prophesied not only the futures of the
twelve sons but also the destinies of the tribes
that would descend from them. For details, see
"Jacob's Blessings" on page 189.

12. What does God do in 49:1-28?

_____

_____

_____

_____

_____

Physicians (50:2). Physicians and embalmers were
two distinct professions in Egypt. Joseph had
his physicians embalm Jacob because the profes-
sional embalmers would have practiced rites
invoking the Egyptian gods in the course of
their work. They believed they were preparing
the dead for afterlife, but Joseph only needed
Jacob's body preserved for the trip to Canaan.
    The embalming took the customary forty
days, and Joseph followed the Egyptian custom
of mourning for seventy days (50:3). Both of
these numbers are attested in Egyptian documents.[10] But Joseph would not have his father
buried in Egypt, and he made his own survivors
promise to move his bones to Canaan someday
(50:5, 24-25).

13. What beliefs and qualities does Joseph display
in 50:1-26?

_____

_____

_____

_____

186

_____

_____

_____

14. Does anything you have learned from the story of Joseph seem relevant to your own life? If so, write down the truth that impresses you and how it is relevant.

_____

_____

_____

_____

_____

_____

_____

15. Is there any way you would like to apply or respond to what you have learned? If so, explain.

_____

_____

_____

_____

_____

_____

_____

16. List any questions you have about 37:1-50:26.

_____

_____

_____

_____

Optional Application: How might the way God repeatedly cared for Joseph while he suffered encourage you to act in your present situation?

Optional Application: a. Set aside a few minutes a day for the next few days to meditate on how God works in the world, and the implications this has for the way you pray and the way you approach life. Write down any implications or plans for action that come to you.

b. Praise God for who He is, and thank Him for the ways He is working through you and other people in the world to accomplish His aims.

For the group

Warm-up. Ask, "What kinds of experiences tempt you to doubt that God is successfully working out a plan for the world and your life?"

Read and summarize.

Questions. This lesson and the next are handled differently from previous ones so that you can look at Joseph's story as a whole. This approach also gives you practice in making lots of observations before you think about interpreting and applying. You may find that not everyone had time to read all fourteen chapters and write answers to so many questions, so you may have to answer some of the observation questions as a group. However, if everyone has already answered questions 1-13, you can make your discussion more interesting by rephrasing the questions: "How is this episode important to the story? What do we learn about God, Joseph, Jacob, and the brothers? How is this episode relevant to us?"

Then give each group member a chance to say how he or she wants to act on some aspect of the story. Be wary of following Joseph's example carelessly; for instance, his masquerade is not necessarily a model for us. Instead, focus on what God does and how Joseph speaks of and responds to God. Your applications may be simply prayer to have Joseph's attitude toward your circumstances or to act as though God is really in control of your life.

Documents from Egypt and the Near East confirm that Genesis accurately portrays customs of Joseph's day. The ornamented robe was a sign of honor. The slave traffic flourished between Egypt, Canaan, and Mesopotamia. It was apparently common for nomads to go to Egypt in times of famine; Egyptian documents record sales of grain to famished herdsmen, and even hospitality to whole tribes when poor rainfall plagued Canaan. The prejudice of Egyptian farmers against nomadic shepherds (whose sheep could wreak havoc with irrigation and graze a field barren in a matter of days) is also well-attested. Even the Egyptian practice of sitting separately at low, round tables (43:32) is portrayed in Egyptian paintings.

Lesson eighteen will deal with chapter 38, so don't spend a lot of time on it.

188

Worship. You began by describing what tempts you to doubt God's faithful care. So, you might end by praising Him for His faithfulness and thanking Him for the witnesses of Scripture and your own experience.

Jacob's Blessings

Most of the blessings in Genesis 49 are prophecies of what would happen to the tribes during the early centuries after the Exodus. The blessing of Judah includes a more distant prophecy.

Reuben lost his birthright for sleeping with his father's concubine (Genesis 35:22). Reuben became a small tribe in the nation of Israel.

Simeon and Levi were both scattered in Israel without their own land because of the massacre at Shechem (Genesis 34). God detested killing for any purpose other than His express command. But while Simeon disintegrated, Levi became the priests and teachers among the other tribes.

With his three elder brothers displaced because of sin, **Judah** became the leader among the southern tribes, and God chose the nation's kings from Judah. Genesis 49:10 points toward the last and true King, the Messiah, who would reign over the other nations as well as Israel. The vines and wine remind one of the intoxicating abundance of the Kingdom of God, the bloody wrath of God's Judgment, and the Blood of Christ represented in the Lord's Supper. Compare Luke 5:33, 7:31-35 and John 2:1-11.

"**Zebulun**'s allotted land in Joshua 19:10-16 did not reach the coast, . . . nor did it closely approach Sidon. But it was near enough to both to be enriched by seaborne trade. . . ." It may also be that Zebulun paid to settle on land dominated by Sidon.

Issachar is portrayed as "a tribe rather too willing to trade its liberty for the material things of life."

Dan means "judge," but Dan chose the "violence and treachery" of Judges 18 as a lifestyle. The tribe is not named in the list of tribes in Revelation 7:5-8.

(continued on page 190)

For Further Study:
What do the blessings in Genesis 49 tell you about God's methods and moral judgments?

Optional Application: Meditate on the way Jacob describes God in 49:24-25. What difference does it make to your life that God is like this? How can you treat Him like this?

(continued from page 189)

Gad was plagued with border raids, but survived.

"With a fertile plain and trade routes to the sea, **Asher** would 'dip his foot in oil' (Deuteronomy 33:24) and produce a notable annual quota for the palace (1 Kings 4:7)."

Naphtali led Israel to break free of bondage (Judges 4-5). "This free, mountainous people" was destined to "breed true, and keep its character."

Joseph's sons, Ephraim and Manasseh, received the best land in Canaan. As Judah led the southern tribes, so they led the northern ones, inheriting the double portion of the firstborn. But their prosperity was brief because of pride (Judges 8:1, 12:1) and apostasy (Hosea 4:17, 5:3-5).

Benjamin was a spirited, violent tribe; see Judges 5:14, 19:1-21:25 and Psalm 68:27.[11]

1. Kidner, page 195; Packer, Tenney, and White, page 117.
2. *The NIV Study Bible,* page 63.
3. Derek Kidner, *Ezra and Nehemiah* (Downers Grove, Illinois: InterVarsity Press, 1979), page 79. (Not cited hereafter.)
4. Kidner, *Genesis,* page 194.
5. Kidner, page 195.
6. de Vaux, pages 129-130.
7. D. Miall Edwards, "Seal," *The International Standard Bible Encyclopaedia,* volume 4, pages 2708-2709.
8. *The NIV Study Bible,* page 69.
9. *The NIV Study Bible,* page 72.
10. Davis, page 19.
11. Kidner, pages 215-222.

GENESIS 37:1-50:26

The Generations of Jacob

Now that you've looked at this narrative once for the plot line and again for more careful observations, you're ready to draw some conclusions. You may want to glance at the Study Skills on pages 39, 63, 91, and 101 first. Use your notes in lesson seventeen to help you answer the questions below.

1. Consider what the teenage Joseph does in 37:2,5-11; he tattles on his older brothers and tells self-exalting dreams to them and even to his father. What does his behavior show about his personality? Does he seem a likely candidate for doing great things in God's service?

   _____

   _____

   _____

   _____

   _____

For Thought and Discussion: Imagine yourself as one of Joseph's brothers. How would you have felt when he announced his dreams?

God working

God was not dependent on Joseph's saintliness to accomplish His aims.

2. Twenty years passed before Joseph's dreams came true (37:2; 41:46,53-54). How did God

191

For Thought and Discussion: How does Joseph's life exemplify Romans 8:28-29?

Optional Application: Did Joseph know God's reasons for what he endured while he was enduring it? (How do you know?) How might this fact affect your response to trials? Pray about this.

For Thought and Discussion: What reasons do we have to believe that God does or does not work in history now as He did in Joseph's day? Support your answer from Scripture.

prepare him to govern Egypt (39:1-23)?

_____

_____

_____

_____

_____

3. God had several purposes in shaping Joseph's life as He did.

a. First, He promised to bless the nations through Abraham's offspring (12:3). How did He use Joseph to give a foretaste of that blessing (41:56-57)?

_____

_____

_____

_____

b. God also promised to protect Jacob and his family (28:13-15). How did he keep that promise in this generation (45:5-7)?

_____

_____

_____

_____

c. God told Abraham that He would let his descendants be enslaved so that He could later liberate them at a pre-planned time (15:13-14). How did He bring about this enslavement in Egypt (45:16-18, 46:1-4)?

_____

_____

_____

192

_____

_____

d. Finally, God wanted to raise up a holy people through the sons of Jacob, but they were jealous, deceptive, vengeful men (34:1-31; 37:4,11,19-20,26-27,31-32). How did God chasten them (42:21, 44:16)?

_____

_____

_____

_____

4. What do God's purposes and actions in the lives of Jacob and his sons tell you about Him?

_____

_____

_____

_____

_____

_____

5. Have you learned anything about God that you want to concentrate and perhaps act on? If so, what is it, and what do you plan to do?

_____

_____

_____

_____

_____

_____

_____

Optional Application: a. Set aside a few minutes a day for the next few days to meditate on how God works in the world and the implications this has for your prayers and actions. Write down any thoughts or decisions that come to you.

b. Praise God for His character, and thank Him for the ways He is working through you and other people in the world.

For Thought and Discussion: The account repeats "The LORD was with Joseph" (39:2,3,21,23) in slavery and prison. What are the implications of this fact for us? Why is it important that God gets the credit for Joseph's successes?

193

For Thought and Discussion: What was good about Joseph's response to temptation in 39:12? Is this tactic something you can practice?

For Thought and Discussion: a. Did Joseph resent his brothers? How can you tell (43:30, 45:1-15)?

b. Was Joseph cruel to deceive his brothers, or did something more than vengeance justify his scheme? Why?

c. What are the dangers of using Joseph's deception as a model for dealing with people who wrong us? Might we ever be justified in doing this? Why or why not?

For Thought and Discussion: Why didn't Joseph succumb to despair in slavery and prison for thirteen years? Does his experience offer you any encouragement?

Jacob and sons

6. Joseph faced repeated temptations during his life. Specifically how did he resist each one? What beliefs, principles, or priorities did he turn to?

the temptation of adultery (39:6-12)

_____

_____

_____

_____

the temptation of pride in his abilities (40:8, 41:16)

_____

_____

_____

_____

the temptation of bitterness and vengefulness against his brothers (45:7-8, 50:19-21)

_____

_____

_____

_____

the temptation to assimilate into Egyptian culture (50:2,22-26)

_____

_____

_____

_____

7. Consider the beliefs and principles you just listed. What similar ones should Christians also have?

_____

_____

_____

_____

_____

_____

8. Like the rest of his family, Joseph also deceived.

   a. How did Joseph's masquerade affect his brothers?

   42:21-22,27-28 _____

   _____

   _____

   _____

   42:37, 43:8-9, 44:18-34 _____

   _____

   _____

   _____

   50:15-18 _____

   _____

   _____

   b. What seems to have been Joseph's purpose for the ruse?

   _____

   _____

   _____

   _____

Optional Application: Are any of the responses to temptation you wrote in questions 6 or 7 relevant to a decision you are facing? If so, how can you apply them?

For Thought and Discussion: Jacob deceived his own father with a slaughtered goat and his brother's clothes (27:9,14-16). Probably without consciously imitating him, his sons tricked him similarly (37:31-33). What principle does this parallel suggest?

Optional Application: Commit yourself to praying daily for awhile that God would develop in you some specific trait that Joseph showed. Look for areas of your life in which you could practice that trait.

195

Optional Application: Is there anyone you need to forgive?

Optional Application: If you are a parent, are you applying the lesson of question 9? Or, do you need to forgive your parents for not applying it?

c. Was Joseph's deception justified? Why or why not?

_____

_____

_____

_____

_____

_____

d. The cycle of deception had been yielding bitter consequences through four generations of Joseph's family. How was this cycle broken (45:4-15, 50:19-21)? (*Optional:* See Matthew 6:12,14-15.)

_____

_____

_____

_____

_____

9. a. How was Jacob like his parents in another way besides deceptiveness (25:28, 37:3)?

_____

_____

_____

b. Consider the results of this trait in each generation (27:1-28:9; 37:4,19-20,26-27). What lesson can we learn from these results?

_____

_____

_____

_____

_____

196

10. Joseph is a type of Christ in some ways. For instance, he was his father's favorite son, was rejected by his brothers, suffered meekly for God's purposes, was delivered and exalted by God, and became the deliverer of the very ones who rejected him.

Why do you think God gave Israel the story of someone whose life resembled what Christ's was going to be? (What does this type tell us about God, His plan, and Scripture?)

For Thought and Discussion: a. Can you think of any other ways in which Joseph's story fore-shadows Christ's?

b. In what ways is Joseph's story differ-ent from Christ's?

For Thought and Discussion: What resulted when Judah married a Canaanite (38:1-10)?

Judah and Tamar (38:1-30)

We skipped over the story of Judah and Tamar until now because it has another point besides just revealing Judah's character. Although it tells us much about customs and moral values among a fallen people, the story's chief purpose is to inform us about the lineage of some important people.

Duty to her as a brother-in-law (38:8). Deuteronomy 25:5-10 explains the law of *levirate marriage* (*levir* is Latin for "brother-in-law").

"The essential purpose [of the levirate marriage was] to perpetuate male descent, the 'name', the 'house' . . . . It was not mere sentiment, but an expression of the importance attached to blood-ties. A secondary, but similar, purpose was to prevent the alienation of family property."

The events of Genesis 38 occurred before the law in Deuteronomy was given, and the story reflects the stricter rules of an even more tribal culture. "The brother-in-law may not decline the duty, and it passes to all the surviving brothers in turn (compare Matthew 22:24-27)." The duty may even have fallen "on the father-in-law if he had no other sons, a practice which is found among some peoples."[1]

For Further Study:
Who were the other
women in Matthew's
genealogy of Jesus:
Rahab (Joshua 2),
Ruth, Uriah's wife
(2 Samuel 11-12),
and Mary? What did
these women have in
common?

**For Thought and
Discussion:** Judah
deceived Tamar; he
never intended to
marry her to Shelah
(38:11). How was her
recompense appro-
priate to his injustice
(38:13-26)?

For Further Study:
Add 37:1-50:26 to
your outline of
Genesis.

11. Read Matthew 1:1-16 (especially verses 3, 6,
    and 16). What does Genesis 38 reveal about the
    ancestry of King David and Jesus Christ?

    _____

    _____

    _____

12. Can you think of anything God might want to
    teach us through this information about Jesus'
    ancestry?

    _____

    _____

    _____

    _____

For the group

Warm-up. Have everyone think of one trial or temptation he or she is currently undergoing. This may
help the group to identify with Joseph and see God's
hand in your lives.

Jacob and sons. Some people feel strongly that
Joseph's deception was as cruel as any other in
Genesis; Jacob nearly died of grief, and Joseph's
brothers lived in terror of him for years. Other
people think God sanctioned this deception, even
though Scripture doesn't say so explicitly. There is
room in question 8c for disagreement, so have
group members justify their interpretations.

If necessary for question 10, refer the group to
the Study Skill on types on page 55. What is the
purpose of types?

Worship. Praise God for being with Joseph in good
times and bad, and for always furthering His own
plan to have mercy on Joseph, his family, and the
starving nations. Praise Him for working out His
plans through your own experiences.

1. de Vaux, pages 37-38.

198

REVIEW

God and Man

At this point, you may have a clear idea of how the themes and plot of Genesis unfold, revealing the nature of God and man. Or, Genesis may be a jumble of stories in your brain or a vague memory of many lessons learned. This review is meant to help you pull the whole book together, to see the story from a God's-eye view. You will probably find yourself paging back to see what you wrote in earlier lessons and leafing back and forth through Genesis.

The best way to begin a review is to reread the whole book at one sitting for major themes. However, because Genesis is so long, we will suggest passages for you to look at.

1. What key things did the story of Creation reveal about God, the world, and humans (1:1-2:25)?

   God _____

   _____

   _____

   _____

   _____

   the world _____

   _____

   _____

_____

_____

humans _____

_____

_____

_____

_____

2. How did the Fall affect people and the world
   (3:1-6:5)? See especially 3:6-19; 4:13-16;
   5:8,11,14; 6:5.

people _____

_____

_____

_____

_____

_____

the world _____

_____

_____

_____

_____

3. What did the events surrounding the Flood
   show about God (6:6-9:17)?

_____

_____

_____

_____

_____

4. What did the Babel crisis show about God and man (11:1-9)?

God _____

_____

_____

_____

_____

man _____

_____

_____

_____

_____

For Thought and Discussion: Summarize what a human being was meant to be and is, according to Genesis.

5. The Flood proved that total destruction was not going to be God's solution to the Fall (8:21). Trace His solution as far as Genesis reveals it.

3:14-24 _____

_____

_____

5:32 _____

_____

_____

9:26, 11:10-27 _____

_____

_____

12:1-3 _____

_____

_____

_____

15:12-21 _____

_____

_____

_____

_____

17:1-16 _____

_____

_____

_____

_____

22:2,8,14 _____

_____

_____

_____

_____

26:1-5 _____

_____

_____

_____

28:10-15, 35:11-13 _____

_____

_____

_____

_____

45:4-13 _____

_____

_____

_____

_____

46:1-4 _____

_____

_____

_____

49:9-12 _____

_____

_____

_____

50:24-25 _____

_____

_____

_____

_____

6. The family of Abraham was far from perfect; deception, violence, and rivalry were frequent. Why is it important that God chose to bless the world and send the Savior through such a family?

_____

_____

_____

_____

_____

Optional Application: To whom could you tell God's plan of redemption as He reveals it in Genesis?

For Thought and Discussion: What is a covenant? Explain the covenants God made with Noah and Abraham. What covenant has He made with Christians?

7. God repeatedly overrode the custom of having eldest sons inherit. He chose Shem over Japheth, Isaac over Ishmael, Jacob over Esau, Joseph and Judah over their brothers, and Ephraim over Manasseh. What is the significance of this pattern?

_____

_____

_____

_____

_____

8. Summarize God's plan to redeem man from the effects of the Fall, to the extent that Genesis reveals that plan.

_____

_____

_____

_____

_____

_____

9. How would you describe God as revealed in Genesis?

_____

_____

_____

_____

_____

_____

_____

_____

10. Hebrews 11 draws chiefly upon Genesis for models of faith. What have Noah, Abraham, and the rest taught you about faith?

_____

_____

_____

_____

_____

_____

11. In the past eighteen lessons you have noted implications that Genesis has for your life. Has your study in any way affected how you think (about yourself, God, other people, circumstances) or act? If so, how?

_____

_____

_____

_____

_____

12. Look back through this study at questions in which you expressed a desire to make some specific application. Consider whether you are satisfied with the results, and how you might continue to pursue growth in those areas. Is there anything you plan to pray about or do?

_____

_____

_____

_____

_____

For Further Study: If you did not write an outline as you went through the book, try outlining Genesis now.

Optional Application:
a. Choose some key passages from Genesis to memorize and meditate upon.
    b. What opportunities for acting or waiting in faith is your life currently offering?
    c. How can the character of God and the nature of man affect the ways you treat people and God this week?

_____

_____

13. Look at the questions about Genesis that you may have listed at the end of each lesson. Has your study answered these questions? If not, do any of the questions still seem important to you? If you do still have significant questions, list them here and consider possible ways of seeking answers. Some of the sources on pages 211-215 may help you.

_____

_____

_____

_____

For the group

Reviewing a big book like Genesis can be hard for several reasons. The discussion can be vague and general because people remember the book only vaguely or have difficulty tying details together to see the big picture. It can also be a dull rehash of what people feel they have already learned.

On the other hand, a review can be an exciting chance to see the story as God sees it, as a whole. The keys to this last result are the attitudes of the leader and the group. The leader needs to motivate the group to want to grasp how the book unfolds. He or she needs to encourage members who find it difficult to connect ideas from many chapters. He or she should urge the group to think ever more deeply about God or man in Genesis, even when quick answers seem to be easy and say everything. At the same time, each group member ought to discipline himself to think and pray to understand more than his own brain finds possible. Seeing the big picture may be difficult, but God's Spirit gives the courage to try and the insight to succeed.

Warm-up. It might be motivating to ask, "What is the most exciting thing you learned about God or yourself from Genesis?" Surely everyone will have

206

learned something that seems important. If you get little response to this question, you could repeat it at the end of your review, after group members' memories have been refreshed.

God and man. You might make a large chart with two columns labeled "God" and "man" for questions 1-4. Then go through each episode of Genesis, having the group list what each shows you about God's character, nature, aims, and methods, and about human nature, purposes, and needs. You should list what human character, nature, etc. were *made to be* and what they *are*. Strive to keep the discussion moving, so that you can finish this discussion in thirty minutes and have time for the rest of the lesson.

Question 9 asks you to pull your comments about God together into a total view of Him. If you've done questions 1-8 carefully, you should be able to describe God richly, to compose a picture that will be the basis of a deeper love for Him. Likewise, the "For Thought and Discussion" on page 201 asks you to pull together your understanding of humanness. This should help you see yourselves. Questions like these should summarize and synthesize, not just repeat, the thoughts you listed. Then, if someone asked you, "How does the Bible (or Genesis) portray God (or man)?" you could answer in a few concise sentences.

Have several people explain God's plan of redemption (question 8). Everyone should listen closely to consider how he or she could explain it more fully or clearly. Again, this is preparation for other questions unbelievers often ask: "What is the Bible about?" or "What is the Old Testament about?" or "Why do Christians think Jesus had to die?"

Question 10 reviews just one theme of Genesis that bears on how Christians ought to live in light of God's nature, man's nature, and God's plan. If each person can name just one insight that truly motivates him, then your study will have been worthwhile. A long list of lessons that don't excite the group will show less success. If the group seems indifferent, try asking someone, "Why is this insight especially motivating to you? How does it move you to act or respond? What difference has it made in your life?" Try to encourage gently.

Application. Questions 11 and 12 are opportunities to review your applications. You could give each person a chance to share one answer to these questions at the end of this meeting. Or if time is running short, save your application review for another meeting in which you will evaluate the study.

When you review your applications, try not to compare your "growth" with each other's, or to focus on guilt and failure. If anyone feels that he has not obeyed God or grown much, you could discuss first whether that is true, and second how the person could approach the situation from now on. The problem may be that the person is focusing on his own efforts rather than on God's nature and power. Or it may be that he has been preoccupied, or has not understood how to respond to what he's learned. Encouragement is the most important gift you can give each other on this issue.

Questions. In this final lesson, give everyone a chance to voice questions about Genesis that remain unanswered. The leader should not answer them himself, but he may point toward books, further study, or other people who could answer the questions. It's a good policy for a leader never to do for the group what it can do for itself.

Evaluation. You might set aside a whole meeting to evaluate your study of Genesis and plan where to go from here. Here are some questions you might consider:

> How well did the study help you grasp the book of Genesis?
> What were the most important truths you learned together about the Lord?
> What did you like best about your meetings?
> What did you like least? What would you change, and how?
> How well did you meet the goals you set at your first meeting?
> What did you learn about small group study?
> How could you together put into practice something you learned from your study?
> What are the members' current needs? What will you do next?

GOING ON IN GENESIS

Ideas for Further Study

1. Go through Genesis, and find all the names given to God (God Most High, the Almighty . . .). Reflect on what they tell you about God's character. If necessary, look them up in a Bible dictionary or Bible encyclopedia to find out what they mean.

2. Find all the types of Christ in Genesis.

3. Trace what you learn about women and/or marriage in Genesis, after the Fall. See, for instance, 3:16-19, 4:19, 12:10-20, 16:1-16, 18:10-15, 19:30-38, 20:1-18, 21:1-21, 23:1-2, 24:1-67, 25:1-6, 25:28, 26:1-11, 27:1-17, 27:41-28:9, 29:1-30:24, 31:14-19, 34:1-31, 38:1-30.

4. Compare gardens: Eden, Gethsemane, the garden of Revelation 21-22. Or, compare cities: Babel, the city of Revelation 21-22.

5. Trace Babylon from Genesis 10:8-12 and 11:1-9, through Isaiah, Jeremiah, Daniel, and Revelation. Use a concordance.

6. Trace the origin and decline of government (1:28, 9:6, 10:8-12, 34:1-31). Look also for signs of rule by authority and by force.

7. Observe the origin and decline of wealth and poverty; of skills, knowledge, and crafts; or of work and toil.

8. Investigate one of these New Testament themes: the pilgrim people, election, grace, the covenant, judgment, righteousness imputed (given) rather than earned, the change of a sinner by grace, paradise, faith, the promises of God.

9. Look for all the "beginnings" in Genesis, such as the origin of language in 11:1-9.

10. Collect the prophecies of Christ in Genesis.

11. Study what Genesis reveals about atonement, and then pursue the subject in Leviticus 16 and in Romans 3.

12. Observe the times when children imitate their parents in Genesis (such as 26:1-11, 34:13-31, 37:31-32). Read some of Paul's letters in the New Testament to see how Christ can break habits inherited from parents.

13. Dreams and visions occur frequently in Genesis and the rest of the Bible. Both (dreams and visions are different) are popular topics of modern speculation. Try tracing how dreams or visions actually figure in God's Word—what they are, who gets them, how God uses them, how they may be abused, what they are not, and so on. You could look up dream(s) or vision(s) in a concordance.

14. Genesis 1 lays to rest the most common human errors about the world: that matter is eternal; that the world of physical things is evil and only the soul is good; that the world came about by chance; that only matter exists, and spiritual things are an illusion; that the world has no purpose; that the stars and planets govern human destiny; that many gods are worthy of worship; that "God" is an impersonal force in all things; that man is just an animal; and many others. Write down how Genesis 1 refutes one or more of these beliefs.

STUDY AIDS

For further information on the material covered in this study, you might consider the following sources. If your local bookstore does not have them, you can have the bookstore order them from the publisher, or you can find them in most seminary libraries. Many university and public libraries will also carry these books.

Commentaries on Genesis

Boice, James Montgomery. *Genesis: An Expositional Commentary* (Zondervan, 2 volumes, 1982).
    Volume 1 covers chapters 1-11 and volume 2 covers chapters 12-50. The books are based on a series of sermons Boice preached, so the focus is on application to modern Christian life. Boice deals with creation versus evolution and evidence for the Flood in readable terms but with plenty of factual research and footnotes for the serious student. At the same time, he explains and applies such ideas as original human nature, fallen human nature, atonement, and salvation in very down-to-earth ways. This book contains deep thinking but is written for the average reader.

Henry, Matthew. *Commentary on the Whole Bible: Volume 1: Genesis-Deuteronomy* (Revell, 1979).
    First published in 1712, this set is unsurpassed in readable, accurate exposition and practical, motivating application. The one-volume abridgment is unreadable, since it merely extracts bits from each section of the original, but the six-volume set is well worth buying or using in a library.

Kidner, Derek. *Genesis* (Tyndale Old Testament Commentaries, InterVarsity Press, 1967).
    An excellent first commentary on Genesis, not exhaustive or overly

scholarly. Kidner includes most of the background a student would need. He also traces the themes of Genesis and often makes connections to modern life. Available in an inexpensive paperback.

Morris, Henry. *The Genesis Record: A Scientific and Devotional Commentary on the Book of Beginnings* (Baker, 1979).
   Morris is a vehement advocate of recent six-day creationism, but he is very fair in explaining the alternate interpretations of Genesis 1. His insights into the nature of man and plan of God make the book worthwhile even for people who are not interested in the controversy about origins.

Old Testament History and Culture

A *history* or *survey* traces Israel's history from beginning to end, so that you can see where each biblical event fits. *A Survey of Israel's History* by Leon Wood (Zondervan, 1970) is a good basic introduction for laymen from a conservative viewpoint. Not critical or heavily learned, but not simplistic. Many other good histories are available.

A **Bible dictionary** or **Bible encyclopedia** alphabetically lists articles about people, places, doctrines, important words, customs, and geography of the Bible.
   The New Bible Dictionary, edited by J.D. Douglas, F.F. Bruce, J.I. Packer, N. Hillyer, D. Gutherie, A.R. Millard, and D.J. Wiseman (Tyndale, 1982) is more comprehensive than most dictionaries. Its 1300 pages include quantities of information along with excellent maps, charts, diagrams, and an index for cross-referencing.
   Unger's Bible Dictionary by Merrill F. Unger (Moody, 1979) is equally excellent and is available in an inexpensive paperback edition.
   The Zondervan Pictorial Encyclopedia edited by Merrill C. Tenney (Zondervan, 1975, 1976) is excellent and exhaustive. It is being revised and updated in the 1980s. However, its five 1000-page volumes are a financial investment, so all but very serious students may prefer to use it at a library.

A good **Bible atlas** can be a great aid to understanding what is going on in a book of the Bible and how geography affected events. Here are a few good choices:
   The MacMillan Atlas by Yohanan Aharoni and Michael Avi-Yonah (MacMillan, 1968, 1977) contains 264 maps, 89 photos, and 12 graphics. The many maps of individual events portray battles, movements of people, and changing boundaries in detail.
   The New Bible Atlas by J.J. Bimson and J.P. Kane (Tyndale, 1985) has 73 maps, 34 photos, and 34 graphics. Its evangelical perspective, concise and helpful text, and excellent research make it a good choice, but its greatest strength is its outstanding graphics, such as cross-sections of the Dead Sea.
   The Bible Mapbook by Simon Jenkins (Lion, 1984) is much shorter and

less expensive than most other atlases, so it offers a good first taste of the usefulness of maps. It contains 91 simple maps, very little text, and 20 graphics. Some of the graphics are computer-generated and intriguing.

The Moody Atlas of Bible Lands by Barry J. Beitzel (Moody, 1984) is scholarly, very evangelical, and full of theological text, indexes, and references. This admirable reference work will be too deep and costly for some, but Beitzel shows vividly how God prepared the land of Israel perfectly for the acts of salvation He was going to accomplish in it.

Yohanan Aharoni has also written *The Land of the Bible: A Historical Geography* (Westminster Press, 1967). After describing the mountains, deserts, winds, rains, and trade routes of ancient Palestine, Aharoni traces the Old Testament history of the promised land with maps and text. For instance, he shows how Abraham lived in Beersheba and how different Judah was from Galilee.

Old Testament Words

A *concordance* lists words of the Bible alphabetically along with each verse in which the word appears. It lets you do your own word studies. An *exhaustive* concordance lists every instance of every word in a given translation. An *abridged* or *complete* concordance omits either some words, some occurrences of the word, or both.

The two best exhaustive concordances are *Strong's Exhaustive Concordance* and *Young's Analytical Concordance to the Bible*. Both are based on the King James Version of the Bible. *Strong's* has an index by which you can find out which Greek or Hebrew word is used in a given English verse. *Young's* breaks up each English-word listing according to the Greek or Hebrew words it translates. Thus, you can cross-reference the original language's words without knowing that language.

Among other good, less expensive concordances, *Cruden's Complete Concordance* is keyed to the King James and Revised Versions, and *The NIV Complete Concordance* is keyed to the New International Version. These include all references to every word included, but they omit "minor" words. They also lack indexes to the original languages.

The Expository Dictionary of the Old Testament, edited by Merrill F. Unger and William White (Thomas Nelson, 1980) defines major biblical Hebrew words. It is not exhaustive, but it is adequate for the average Bible student who does not know Hebrew.

For Small Group Leaders

The Small Group Leader's Handbook by Steve Barker et. al. (InterVarsity, 1982).

Written by an InterVarsity small group with college students primarily in mind. It includes more than the above book on small group dynamics and how to lead in light of them, and many ideas for worship, building community, and outreach. It has a good chapter on doing inductive Bible study.

Getting Together: A Guide for Good Groups by Em Griffin (InterVarsity, 1982). Applies to all kinds of groups, not just Bible studies. From his own experience, Griffin draws deep insights into why people join groups; how people relate to each other; and principles of leadership, decision making, and discussions. It is fun to read, but its 229 pages will take more time than the above book.

You Can Start a Bible Study Group by Gladys Hunt (Harold Shaw, 1984). Builds on Hunt's thirty years of experience leading groups. This book is wonderfully focused on God's enabling. It is both clear and applicable for Bible study groups of all kinds.

How to Build a Small Groups Ministry by Neal F. McBride (NavPress, 1994). This hands-on workbook for pastors and lay leaders includes everything you need to know to develop a plan that fits your unique church. Through basic principles, case studies, and worksheets, McBride leads you through twelve logical steps for organizing and administering a small groups ministry.

How to Lead Small Groups by Neal F. McBride (NavPress, 1990). Covers leadership skills for all kinds of small groups—Bible study, fellowship, task, and support groups. Filled with step-by-step guidance and practical exercises to help you grasp the critical aspects of small group leadership and dynamics.

DJ Plus, a special section in *Discipleship Journal* (NavPress, bimonthly). Unique. Three pages of this feature are packed with practical ideas for small groups. Writers discuss what they are currently doing as small group members and leaders. To subscribe, write to Subscription Services, Post Office Box 54470, Boulder, Colorado 80323-4470.

Bible Study Methods

Braga, James. *How to Study the Bible* (Multnomah, 1982). Clear chapters on a variety of approaches to Bible study: synthetic, geographical, cultural, historical, doctrinal, practical, and so on. Designed to help the ordinary person without seminary training to use these approaches.

Fee, Gordon, and Douglas Stuart. *How to Read the Bible For All Its Worth* (Zondervan, 1982). After explaining in general what interpretation (exegesis) and application (hermneneutics) are, Fee and Stuart offer chapters on interpreting and applying the different kinds of writing in the Bible: Epistles, Gospels, Old Testament Law, Old Testament narrative, the Prophets, Psalms, Wisdom, and Revelation. Fee and Stuart also suggest good commentaries on each biblical book. They write as evangelical scholars who personally recognize Scripture as God's Word for their daily lives.

Jensen, Irving L. *Independent Bible Study* (Moody, 1963), and *Enjoy Your Bible* (Moody, 1962).
   The former is a comprehensive introduction to the inductive Bible study method, especially the use of synthetic charts. The latter is a simpler introduction to the subject.

Wald, Oletta. *The Joy of Discovery in Bible Study* (Augsburg, 1975).
   Wald focuses on issues such as how to observe all that is in a text, how to ask questions of a text, how to use grammar and passage structure to see the writer's point, and so on. Very helpful on these subjects.

Titles in the LifeChange series:

Genesis (#9069X)
Exodus (#92838)
Joshua (#91211)
Ruth & Esther (#90746)
1 Samuel (#92773)
Proverbs (#93486)
Isaiah (#91114)
Matthew (#99964)
Mark (#99107)
Luke (#99301)
John (#92374)
Acts (#91122)
Romans (#90738)
1 Corinthians (95594)
2 Corinthians (#99514)

Galatians (#95624)
Ephesians (#90541)
Philippians (#9072X)
Colossians/Philemon (#9119X)
1 Thessalonians (#99328)
2 Thessalonians (#99921)
1 Timothy (#99530)
2 Timothy (#99956)
Titus (#99115)
Hebrews (#92722)
James (#91203)
1 Peter (#90525)
2 Peter and Jude (#99948)
1, 2, & 3 John (#91149)
Revelation (#92730)

ACKNOWLEDGMENTS

The LIFECHANGE series has been produced through the coordinated efforts of a team of Navigator Bible study developers and NavPress editorial staff, along with a nationwide network of fieldtesters.

SERIES EDITOR: KAREN LEE-THORP